The New Heart of Hong Kong

The New Heart of Hong Kong

INTERNATIONAL COMMERCE CENTRE

ORO EDITIONS

Published by
ORO editions
Publishers of Architecture, Art, and Design
Gordon Goff: Publisher
www.oroeditions.com
info@oroeditions.com

ISBN: 978-1-935935-74-2

10 09 08 07 06 5 4 3 2 1 First edition

Edited by: Rebecca Lo
Managing Editor: Jake Anderson

Book Design:
Pablo Mandel / CircularStudio.com

Color Separations and Printing: ORO Group Ltd.
Printed in China.

This book was printed and bound using a variety of sustainable manufacturing processes and materials including soy-based inks, acqueous-based varnish, VOC- and formaldehyde-free glues, and phthalate-free laminations. The text is printed using offset sheetfed lithographic printing process in (book specific) color on 157gsm premium matt art paper with an off-line gloss acqueous spot varnish applied to all photographs.

ORO editions makes a continuous effort to minimize the overall carbon footprint of its publications. As part of this goal, ORO editions, in association with Global ReLeaf, arranges to plant trees to replace those used in the manufacturing of the paper produced for its books. Global ReLeaf is an international campaign run by American Forests, one of the world's oldest nonprofit conservation organizations. Global ReLeaf is American Forests' education and action program that helps individuals, organizations, agencies, and corporations improve the local and global environment by planting and caring for trees.

For information on our distribution, please visit our website www.oroeditions.com

CONTENTS

FOREWORD

Courtesy: Sun Hung Kai Properties

This is the story of how Hong Kong came to acquire one of the most impressive and recognisable icons of architecture and engineering along the world famous Victoria Harbour shoreline. It has its origins in the rise of Sun Hung Kai Properties from its modest beginnings to becoming a powerhouse in what is possibly the most dynamic city in Asia for business, finance and real estate development.

Sun Hung Kai Properties (SHKP) was founded by the late Kwok Tak Seng and two friends in the 1960s. The company soon became a leader in the local property market with its innovative products and emphasis on quality. The 60s and 70s were tumultuous times in Hong Kong but Mr. Kwok always maintained his faith in the territory's future. This confidence paid off handsomely in the years to come.

Mr. Kwok and his friends went their separate business ways by the early 70s. In 1972, Mr. Kwok set up Sun Hung Kai Properties (SHKP) and listed it publicly the same year. The fledgling company saw vast potential in the hitherto underdeveloped New Territories and began acquiring land there. One of its first major mixed use projects was Tsuen Wan Centre, followed by the joint-venture Shatin City One and later New Town Plaza in Shatin.

SHKP retained its faith in Hong Kong despite political uncertainty and pressed ahead with premium developments such as Central Plaza in Wan Chai, which was Hong Kong's tallest building at the time it was completed.

Kwok Tak Seng passed away in 1990 at the age of 79 and the next generation of the Kwok family took over the SHKP reins. The company's business strategy remained the same, with the Hong Kong property market the main focus of operations. At the same time, it expanded its portfolio vertically and formed internal departments for architecture, construction and project management, as well as support services for its property development business.

Still, the company's faith in Hong Kong continued. SHKP completed International Finance Centre in Central in 1998, followed by 2IFC in 2003. It then made another bold move when it acquired the site for International Commerce Centre, which overtook 2IFC to become the territory's tallest building in 2011.

The story of ICC that follows is a remarkable tale of engineering, innovation confidence and vision, but SHKP is not content to rest on its laurels. It continues to build Hong Kong and construct even newer landmark developments in mainland China. Read on to find out how Hong Kong building history was made.

EST KOWLOON CULTURAL DISTR

PREFACE

Hong Kong is a world-renowned city, a beacon to many people, and a gateway to mainland China and Asia for national and international commerce. Central has long been the business centre for Hong Kong. Standing tall in the centre of it is International Finance Centre, watching over Kowloon.

Across Victoria Harbour, in Kowloon, standing high above all surrounding buildings is International Commerce Centre (ICC). It stands as a pillar of the gateway to Hong Kong along with International Finance Centre.

International Commerce Centre stands as a new symbol for Hong Kong, and is the centre of the new financial district in Kowloon. A half hour train ride from the airport, a central hub of the MTR, and, with the construction of a bullet train/Express Rail Link that will connect it to neighboring Guangzhou ICC is truly the new heart of Hong Kong – the hub to, from, and through the city. It stands as a welcoming monument to the growth and future development of this thriving metropolis.

1/

THE NEW HEART OF HONG KONG

King Wai Lo was extremely agitated on the inside but he was careful not to show any emotion on the outside. Sun Hung Kai Properties Real Estate Agency's general manager (Office Leasing) was doing the deal of his life and it came down to the wire: give up valuable rental space in International Commerce Centre (ICC) for a plant room or the anchor tenant, a global banking leader, was not signing. He took a deep breath, did some quick calculations in his head, and said ok.

In the developer-driven world of Hong Kong real estate, Lo's play was unprecedented. "This sacrifice on our part became a decent return in the end," Lo says, explaining his rationale. "In the beginning, we had to make sacrifices. Sure, we could have targeted lower profile companies as potential tenants. But we knew what a special building we had."

"We work on a lot of commercial projects," says H.K. Yung, director with J. Roger Preston, the mechanical and electrical (M&E) consulting engineers on ICC. "For this project, we changed a lot of office space into M&E areas. That cost a lot of money. Normally, M&E is gross floor area (GFA) that is non-accountable. In the end, we needed to meet the anchor tenants' requirements. We needed to gain their trust, whether it was by providing additional generators, chillers or whatever they needed to do their business. Some may have needed half a floor changed into M&E space. That GFA is very expensive. I don't think in 30 years of working in Hong Kong had I ever done this before."

Considering that the land ICC stands upon was a typhoon shelter only a dozen years ago, the building is even more remarkable.

Central has historically been where Hong Kong executives have always conducted business. Even its name refers to it being the city's central business district (CBD), as it was where intrepid entrepreneurs sailing into Hong Kong on clipper ships first set up their warehouses more than 150 years ago—only a stone's throw away from where the British marked their new territory on Possession Point.

By the 1970s, the nature of business had changed and the city's Victorian colonnaded architecture was slowly replaced by high rise buildings, starting with Jardine House (formerly known as Connaught Centre) by Jim Kinoshita of Palmer and Turner Architects & Engineers (P&T) in 1972. From its trading roots, Hong Kong became an industrial

Above, left to right:
Jardine House, designed by Jim Kinoshita of Palmer & Turner, paved the way for the successively taller skyscrapers that began to dominate Central's skyline in the 1970s. Its distinctive porthole shaped windows are said to resemble good luck coins for owner Jardine Matheson, one of Hong Kong's oldest companies.

The Shek Kip Mei fire on Christmas day 1953 was a wake up call for the Hong Kong government and spurred the first series of public housing estates to meet the tide of incoming refugees predominantly from mainland China.

Sha Tin prior to reclamation in the late 1960s was a sparsely populated hilly area in eastern New Territories. Its proximity to Kowloon made it ideal as Hong Kong's first planned satellite city.

Opposite page:
Sha Tin in the early 1980s was already a thriving "new town" with a combination of public and private housing, schools, services such as markets and libraries, and infrastructure including public transportation via rail and an extensive bus network.

centre in the post World War II era, and then a service-oriented society when those industries moved north into the Pearl River Delta in the 1980s as China began opening its doors. The CBD's towers, each higher, more high tech and more expensive than its predecessor, began to reflect a service-oriented economy, with banks, insurance companies and law firms taking over from shipping companies and others who did not require a prestigious Central address on their business cards.

At the same time, Hong Kong was swelling from successive waves of immigrants from the Chinese mainland. The Shek Kip Mei shanty town fire on Christmas day in 1953, which left 53,000 people homeless, underscored not only the urgent need for public housing, but also that businesses needed diversification. New self-contained towns needed to be set up for people to live, work and play, easing the already congested arteries facilitating daily workers heading back and forth from Central.

Ling Kar Kan is the past president of The Hong Kong Institute of Planners and a director in the Planning Department of the Government of the Hong Kong Special Administrative Region (HKSAR). "In the late 70s and early 80s, when people looked at the problems of the world, they tend to conceptualize it as being a problem of cities," Ling says. "If we could resolve urban problems, we could solve the problems of the world. At that time, the most pressing problems were in the big cities: slums, poor living conditions, rural migration that brought about every sort of housing, hygiene and health issues, not to mention sociological problems such as alienation. This was also reflected in Hong Kong. In the late 1970s, we started the new town programme. As a first year geography student, I went to Sha Tin old town and witnessed how it was

Right, left to right:
The Kai Tak International Airport terminal building was one of Eric Cumine's many projects in Hong Kong. A Eurasian originally from Shanghai, Cumine was one of the city's most prolific architects from the 50s to 70s.

Kai Tak's two runways extended into Kowloon Bay and were built at a time when eastern Kowloon was dominated by warehouses. As the city mushroomed, the height restrictions imposed on buildings in Kowloon transformed neighbourhoods into dense urban areas of uniform height.

Below, top to bottom:
The north Lantau island of Chek Lap Kok was earmarked for a new and much larger airport by Governor David Wilson as part of his proposed "Rose Garden" project.

Hong Kong International Airport was designed by Lord Norman Foster to be a state-of-the-art facility that set the benchmark for Asian airports to come.

Opposite page, left to right:
The Hong Kong and Shanghai Banking Corporations replaced its former Art Deco head office building in Central with a tower designed by Lord Norman Foster opened in 1985.

Central's skyline in the 1950s was a combination of colonnaded Victorian warehouses and Art Deco buildings, with the Star Ferry plying the waters between Hong Kong and Kowloon.

demolished to make way for a new town's development. I saw how urban planning would make a significant contribution to Hong Kong, and that we needed urban renewal, town planning and public housing."

After Sha Tin, new towns were rolled out in succession across the New Territories concurrently with the rapid urban development of north Hong Kong island and the streets surrounding Nathan Road in Tsim Sha Tsui. Mass migration in the 70s, 80s and 90s alarmed the government enough so that it fast-tracked plans for a massive infrastructure project dubbed Port and Airport Development Strategy. The city's increasing amount of flights meant that the two runways at Kai Tak Airport were far from sufficient to meet demand, and an island northeast of Lantau was earmarked as the ideal place for a new airport. Chek Lap Kok stood at the center of what was nicknamed the Rose Garden project. The master plan would yield a new town adjacent to the airport—Tung Chung—and also make airport transfers into Central easy and convenient along a new Mass Transit Rail (MTR) line.

Ken Shuttleworth, former partner with Foster & Partners and founder of his own London-based firm Make Architects established in 2004, moved to Hong Kong in the late 1970s to oversee work on HSBC bank headquarters and the airport at Chek Lap Kok. "We always knew that Rose Garden was the plan," he recalls. "When I was working on HSBC in Central, we were restricted to a height of 180 metres because the building was in the flight path of planes from Kai Tak. HSBC's height was the maximum until that air route was moved. That was how I.M. Pei was able to build Bank of China higher than HSBC. But we all knew that all the heights of buildings in Kowloon would go up as soon as the airport

moved. And it presented a great opportunity to re-make Kowloon."

"Many cities grow organically," says Valerie Portefaix, co-founder of MAP Office and Master of Design lecturer at The Hong Kong Polytechnic University's School of Design. "Hong Kong plans its public transport first, with a straight line from one destination to another. And then it fills in the gaps."

"Governor David Wilson (1987-1992) first came up with the idea for the Rose Garden," recalls David Lung, former dean and currently Lady Edith Kotewall Professor in the Built Environment at The University of Hong Kong's Faculty of Architecture. "There was talk in Hong Kong just before and after the handover of it being part of a larger metropolis that would include Shenzhen, Macau and Zhuhai. In that scenario, the entire CBD would move north. There would be a centre in Mongkok and Prince Edward. I was on the Town Planning Board in 1991. Even then, Sun Hung Kai Properties was farsighted enough to plan a strategy for developing southern Kowloon. It knew that once the airport height restrictions were lifted from 20 storeys, it could develop much taller buildings. ICC is the result of its strategy. They were able to anticipate what could happen in the future. Central is too far from Shenzhen. That's why the Express Rail Link (XRL) is planned for West Kowloon."

As soon as travellers realised that they cut their time to 26 minutes from the Hong Kong International Airport (HKIA) to Central via Airport Express, everyone began to take the MTR link—even those who only previously made airport transfers by limousine. The smaller percentage of people whose final destination was in Kowloon made use of the Kowloon stop along the line, at a time when the station was the only thing in the new West Kowloon reclaimed district.

"Kowloon Station, the development above the Airport Express Station in Kowloon, was originally envisioned as a secondary business centre extending from Tsim Sha Tsui according to the city's strategic plans," says Margaret Chan, a senior development manager with Sun Hung Kai Properties. "It wasn't conceived to be the expansion of Central's CBD then. In former Chief Executive Tung Chee Hwa's first policy address in 1998, he outlined the vision of Hong Kong being an Asian financial centre. To realise this dream, Hong Kong needed more world class offices. In the same year, the Rose Garden Airport Core Project moved the airport to Lantau. And with Airport Express, the travelling distance made HKIA very close to the Metro Area. You could literally step out of the airport and be in the city within minutes. Kowloon Station was also created as a transportation hub transacted by two rail links and a public transport terminus, with another rail link and cross harbour tunnel at its door. The XRL now under construction is an added bonus." Not only was travel time cut, but the entire journey was made more comfortable as the Airport Express offers a smooth and reliable ride on dedicated tracks unencumbered by vehicular traffic.

As an iconic building capping XRL, ICC stands as a beacon both literally and symbolically welcoming travellers to China. Together with International Finance Centre (IFC) across Victoria Harbour, they form the gateway towers that signal safe passage, whether it is a first or the 10,000th journey in the harbour. In keeping with Hong Kong being the world's first east meets west city, the two towers also allude to the homecoming concept that inspired J.R.R. Tolkien more than 70 years

ago—and what became *The Two Towers*, the title of the second volume in his *The Lord of the Rings* trilogy. The dual notions of coming home and beginning a journey, with physical markers to designate a doorway, is something that ICC's New York City-based architect Kohn Pedersen Fox (KPF) had in mind from the outset. Many hours, numerous consultants and countless sleepless nights transformed what was supposed to be just another office block into the district nucleus that ICC is today. As ICC is a building in flux, with XRL and West Kowloon Cultural District still to be built to complete the site, its evolution is something that the entire city—and many beyond—await eagerly.

Above:
Reclamation of West Kowloon included the construction of a third cross harbour tunnel connecting Hong Kong island with the Kowloon peninsula.

Right:
International Commerce Centre, designed by New York City-based architect Kohn Pedersen Fox, acts like a light beacon at night. Together with International Finance Centre in Central, the two form a symbolic gateway to China.

Hong Kong Architecture: The Fifth Wave

The city's architectural development can be roughly categorised into five distinct periods, although there are new buildings erected in the style of previous periods by developers and architects who hanker for days of yore. Rather than distinct stops and starts, architectural movements in Hong Kong are akin to tidal waves, where old sit beside new both happily and incongruously.

We, none of us, can escape our past. A city's architecture chronicles that past to anyone who experiences it, whether it is via photography, film, or in person. A city such as Hong Kong, with its humble origins as China's most southern frontier, got an architectural kick start through English colonisation. With each successive wave of political and cultural movements affecting Hong Kong's way of life, its architects reflected those forces through their work. Local and international firms were inspired to push the envelope with groundbreaking buildings that shaped and continue to shape the city's skyline. The waves that affected architecture can be discerned through carefully peeling back the layers. They are evident across the territory in Central's business district, filtering down to various neighbourhoods and suburban areas.

—David Lung, Lady Edith Kotewall Professor in the Built Environment at The University of Hong Kong's Faculty of Architecture

Prior to 1860, or when the Chinese island of Hong Kong was ceded to the British, architecture remained domestic or sacred; houses and temples bore similarities to each other and the central courtyard was a dominant feature in both. With the rapid development of Hong Kong as a port of trade (above), commercial and then institutional architecture began to drive the direction of what the city's urban landscape looked like.

First Wave:
1860 onwards; Chinese Hong Kong became British Hong Kong

ARCHITECTURAL STYLE: Colonial English; noteworthy buildings include St. John's Cathedral (above), Murray House, The Peninsula Hotel (opposite page, below) and Tai O Police Station (left)
ARCHITECTS: English firms that originated in Shanghai; noteworthy architects include Palmer & Turner (P&T) and Leigh & Orange (L&O)
DEVELOPMENT: mostly concentrated on the north shore of Hong Kong island in Central, with a few developments scattered across the territory as need arose for new buildings

Second Wave:
1955 onwards; the year when The University of Hong Kong's (HKU) first batch of architecture students graduated

ARCHITECTURAL STYLE: International Style tempered by local inspiration; noteworthy buildings include Jackson Wong's private residence in Chung Hom Kok (above), Donald Liao's Wah Fu Public Housing Estate (left), Eric Cumine's Kai Tak International Airport
ARCHITECTS: emergence of Hong Kong architects who studied under Raymond Gordon Brown, HKU's first dean of architecture; noteworthy architects include Jackson Wong, Ng Chun Man and Donald Liao; spread of HKU architects to North America, including Gus da Roza and Michael McDougall
DEVELOPMENT: Hong Kong island, Kowloon up to Boundary Street

Third Wave:
1975 onwards; the Cross Harbour Tunnel (above left) opened, linking Hung Hom to Causeway Bay by road; it was quickly followed by the launch of MTR's (top) Island Line

ARCHITECTURAL STYLE:
International Style mixed with Postmodernism and Deconstructivism; noteworthy buildings include P&T's Jardine House, Wong Ouyang's Pacific Place (above right), Foster & Partners' HSBC Bank Headquarters, I.M. Pei's Bank of China Tower
ARCHITECTS: emergence of the composite firm; noteworthy architects include Jim Kinoshita of P&T, Lam Wo Hei of Wong & Ouyang, Dennis Lau of Dennis Lau Ng Chun Man and Edward Ho of Wong Tung locally; British and American architects making iconic statements include Foster & Partners, I.M. Pei
DEVELOPMENT: redevelopment of Central, attempts at CBD diversification to Causeway Bay, Taikoo and Tsim Sha Tsui

Fourth Wave:
1997 onwards; British Hong Kong becomes Chinese Hong Kong; Asian Financial Crisis

ARCHITECTURAL STYLE:
Neopostmodernism, return to Bauhaus principles, pseudo Mediterranean villa residences; noteworthy buildings includes Wong & Ouyang's Hong Kong Convention & Exhibition Centre Phase II (top), Arquitectonica's Festival Walk (above), Leo Daly's Cheung Kong Centre, Cesar Pelli's 2IFC
ARCHITECTS: international firms with local presence alongside local firms with international practices; noteworthy architects include Rocco Yim, Steve Leung, Moira Moser, KPF, OMA, Aedas
DEVELOPMENT: gentrification of industrial areas such as Taikoo, urban renewal projects such as Wanchai's Wedding Card Street, heritage preservation projects such as Bethanie (right)

Fifth Wave:
2011 onwards; intensified development of reclaimed land and gentrification projects

ARCHITECTURAL STYLE: Academically-oriented experimentation, hospitality-driven design; noteworthy buildings include Rocco Yim's Central Government Offices (right), KPF's ICC, Tod William Billie Tsien's Asia Society Hong Kong Center

ARCHITECTS: boutique firms with an emphasis on strong interior design; noteworthy architects include Neri & Hu, Andre Fu, One Plus Partnership
DEVELOPMENT: West Kowloon, Aberdeen, Kwai Chung, Kwun Tong

(BELOW)
Wong & Ouyang has steadily contributed to the increasing growth of Hong Kong's skyline for the past five decades

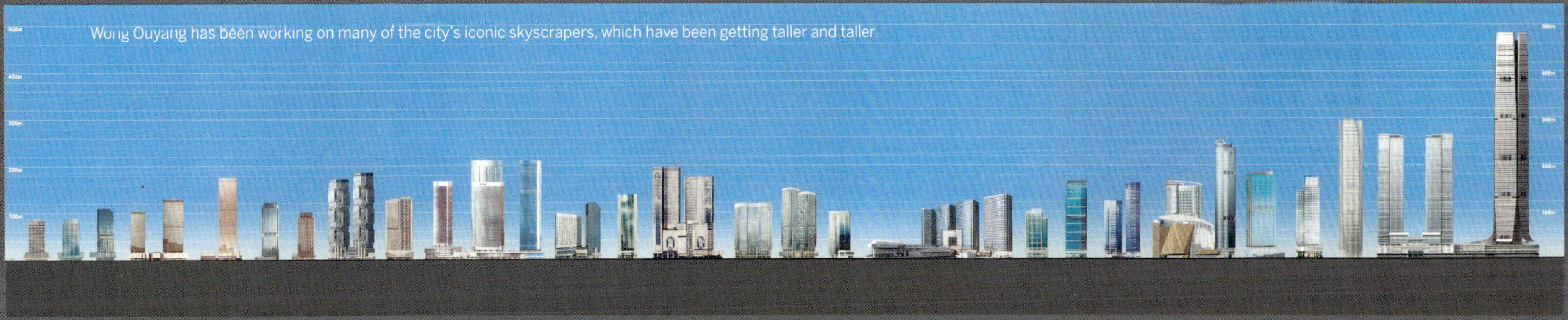

2/

LAYING THE GROUNDWORK

One of ICC's key strengths is its location. The building's story may be summarised as how a former typhoon shelter is transformed into a financial hub. And it all started because of Hong Kong's pressing need for a new airport.

By the 1980s, it was clear that Kai Tai Airport's two runways jutting out into Kowloon Bay were inadequate to handle the millions of passengers and freight flowing through the former colony every year. When it first opened in the late 1920s, Kai Tak was far removed from residential areas. Yet by the 1960s and as the result of successive waves of migrants mostly from across the border, both the city and the airport's expansion brought them dangerously close to each other.

Many passengers arriving in Hong Kong can still recall the harrowing experience of flying increasingly closer to bamboo poles of laundry protruding from residential blocks. In order to get to and from Kai Tak, travellers were restricted to taxis or cars, as there was no Mass Transit Rail (MTR) connecting the airport to urban destinations. The result was heavy traffic congestion in the east Kowloon area regardless of the time of day. Kai Tak was also impeding the development of the area, as buildings within the airport's flight path were restricted to 180 metres. With buildable land scarce, the only way was to go up. Hong Kong was bursting at the seams and the search for the ideal location to house an international calibre airport was on.

After considering a number of sites, the island of Chek Lap Kok north of Lantau island was chosen. Not wanting to make the same mistake as Kai Tak with an airport that no one could conveniently access, a comprehensive strategy was devised. The Airport Core Programme consisted of 10 parts, with transportation being one of its key components. Already on its way to becoming a leader in Asian efficiency, the Hong Kong government knew that moving the airport 30 kilometres west of Kai Tak meant that it had to be extremely well connected with urban areas. That meant not only rail but also vehicular arteries needed to be completed to make getting to Chek Lap Kok just as quick and convenient as to Kowloon Bay, if not easier.

Above: Taken in November 2008 a couple of years before completion from the upper floors of ICC looking north, the relocated Yau Ma Tei Typhoon Shelter can be seen sharing the harbour with numerous new residential developments.

Opposite page: ICC and the luxury highrise residences at Union Square make up a hub that is conveniently located within close proximity to land and sea transportation arteries.

In June 1992, Hong Kong governor David Wilson directed the Town Planning Board to prepare a plan for reclaiming the southwestern part of the Kowloon Peninsula. The plan followed a report prepared in 1983 by the Harbour Reclamation and Urban Growth that recommended the development of West Kowloon. It would provide land for transportation infrastructure via airport rail, roads and a new harbour crossing, as well as to help relieve the congested districts in Central Kowloon, namely Tsim Sha Tsui, Yau Ma Tei and Mongkok.

The West Kowloon reclamation was considered the most complicated of the 10 components that made up the Airport Core Programme, according to a 2004 report by Ho Pui Yin entitled *Challenges for an Evolving City: 160 Years of Port and Land Development in Hong Kong*. An additional 334 hectares will be created, increasing the size of Kowloon peninsula by a third. It would encompass the territory from Tsim Sha Tsui to Cheung Sha Wan and Mei Foo. It would entail the development of two MTR stations: what eventually became Kowloon and Olympic. 120 hectares of the land was designated to be used for the West Kowloon Expressway, a new highway directly linking the airport with the Western Harbour Crossing that bypasses the city itself.

Left: ICC's neighbours are dominated by high end condos and apartments above Kowloon Station, attracting residents with higher education, income brackets and spending power to raise the peninsula's profile.

Opposite page: In November 2008, the various phases of ICC can be seen as the lower floors were fully operational even as the upper floors were being constructed.

Following pages: During a sunset, the northwestern façade of ICC takes on a dramatic glow enhanced by the lights of the city.

ICBC 工银亚洲
熱烈祝賀

Opposite page: Within the residential complex above Kowloon Station, ICC's dragon tail extension transforms into an open public plaza dubbed Civic Square.

Above: In March 2009, the still under construction ICC dominates the West Kowloon skyline like a signpost guiding travellers across the sea.

The reclamation was completed in three phases. The first was to relocate the Yau Ma Tei Typhoon Shelter further south and west, opening up the area to be reclaimed in 1990. The final phase involved reclaiming 13 hectares at the very south of West Kowloon, which was completed by 1997. With MTRC as the landlord, Kowloon Station opened in 1998, providing a direct high speed rail link to the airport. It also offers an in-town check-in service similar to its sister facility in Central that allows passengers to save time by dropping off their baggage before heading to the airport.

"With the airport rail, travelling times are reduced to within the metropolitan area," says Margaret Chan with Sun Hung Kai Properties. "That's where you have the gateway. The travel time between the airport and the city is now a short and pleasantly scenic train ride. Kowloon Station was planned to be a transportation hub."

The Town Planning Board approved a revised master layout plan in 1995 for the trapezoidal shaped parcel of land directly above Kowloon Station to consist of six commercial towers ranging from 30 to 70 storeys and 18 residential towers ranging from 30 to 55 storeys. This number was in line with the original 1983 study for the West Kowloon reclamation to improve the living standards in the district. Further revised master layout plans amalgamated the commercial floor areas into an iconic office tower. ICC was the last part of Kowloon Station's development, with the hotel the final component open in 2011.

Within the 10 year period from when Sun Hung Kai Properties was awarded the contract to build the iconic commercial tower above Kowloon Station in September 2000 to when The Ritz-Carlton, Hong

Left: A number of al fresco dining and drinking options are available at Civic Square, conveniently at the foot of ICC above Elements shopping mall.

Opposite page: Civic Square above Kowloon station includes lush landscaping and skylights illuminating the mall below; it acts as a welcoming green carpet for ICC.

Kong opened for business in March 2011, the economic makeup of West Kowloon had undergone a remarkable transformation. While east Kowloon, specifically near the former airport, saw its share of new high rise developments and gentrification of industrial buildings, West Kowloon's developments around Kowloon and Olympic Stations have been predominantly high end or upper mid end—such as ICC, the two hotels W and The Ritz-Carlton, Hong Kong, and the adjacent luxury residences above Kowloon Station. Consequently, the district has attracted residents with better education, higher income brackets and increased spending power. These high net worth individuals have tipped the district, even going as far as raising Kowloon peninsula's profile.

According to census data from 2001 and 2011, education levels attained by residents in the Yau Tsim Mong district shot up from 16.4% to 32.4% for post-secondary grads, in comparison to an increase from 14.5% to 24.9% for the whole of Kowloon. "The changes have been drastic," says Chan. "After the establishment of ICC—from 2008 onwards, which can be interpreted from the census data as the period from 2006 to 2011 inclusive, primary level only attainment decreased 9.5%. However, secondary level only attainment decreased about 5% and post-secondary level attainment increased 16%. This shows that ICC, as a prominent centre for employment, has contributed a greater inflow of more educated people in the district."

The median monthly household income of people living in the district has seen even more amazing changes. In 2001, census shows the median household income for Yau Tsim Mong to be HK$14,705 while by 2011, it was HK$22,070. That compares to a less significant change for Kowloon on the whole, which went from a median of HK$15,850 in 2001 to HK$18,020 in 2011. More telling is the median household income of HK$99,000 for residents at Kowloon Station, for the first time a distinct number in 2011.

"The increase in contribution by high end level services such as managers and professionals has been increasing, especially after ICC," notes Chan. "It shows that ICC influences the proportion of different occupations in the district, weighing more and more onto high end level services." The number of Yau Tsim Mong managers and professionals increased from 31.13% in 2001 to 43.56% in 2011, impacting the whole of Hong Kong which went up from 31.61% in 2001 to 36.24% in 2011. At the same time, people working in construction and manufacturing in Yau Tsim Mong decreased from 12,213 and 13,201 in 2001 to 10,377 and 5,355 in 2011 respectively. This was most likely due to the slow down in construction within the area and industrial activity moving further north in search of lower rents.

"The social economic impact of ICC upon West Kowloon has had a positive effect on the community," says Chan. "Not too many major developments in the Yau Tsim Mong district would have brought about such a major change."

What makes the transformation even more remarkable is that a decade ago the geographical area didn't even exist. Today, West Kowloon is arguably a financial powerhouse in its own right that gives Central a run for its money.

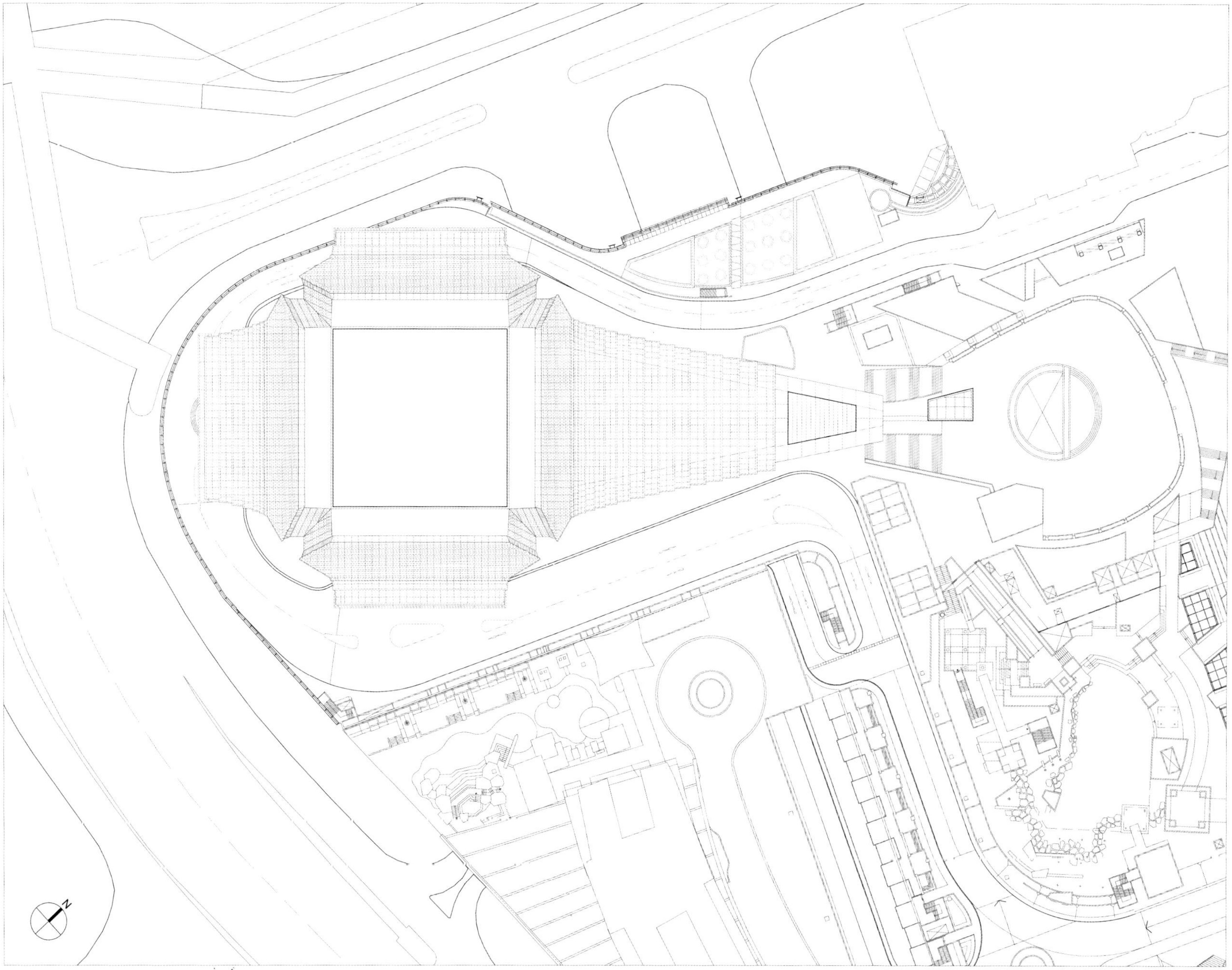

Opposite page: The plan of West Kowloon in relation to Tsim Sha Tsui and Central shows that ICC and 2IFC are strategically situated directly across Victoria Harbour from each other to form a pair of beacons marking a gateway to the city.

Above: A top view of ICC shows that it is conveniently situated near the entrance to the West Harbour Tunnel as well as being connected to the city's extensive road network.

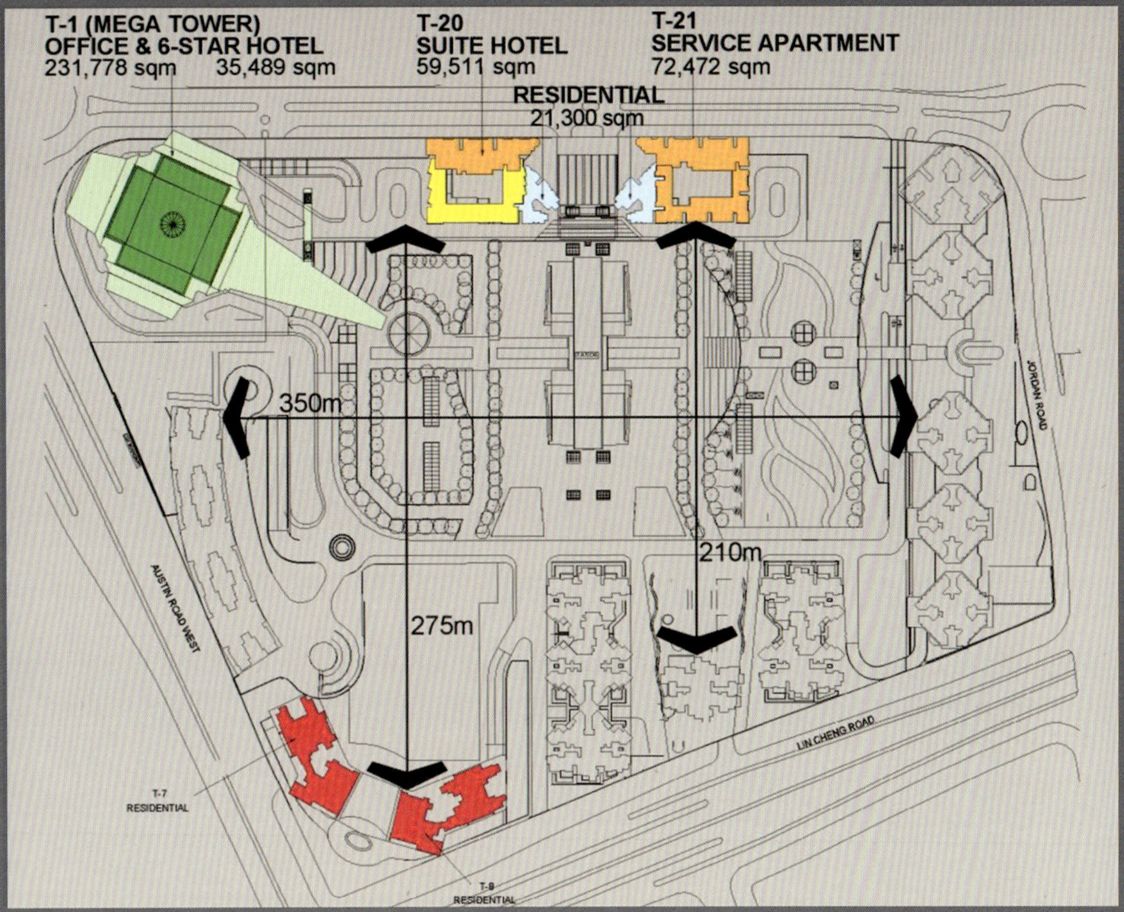

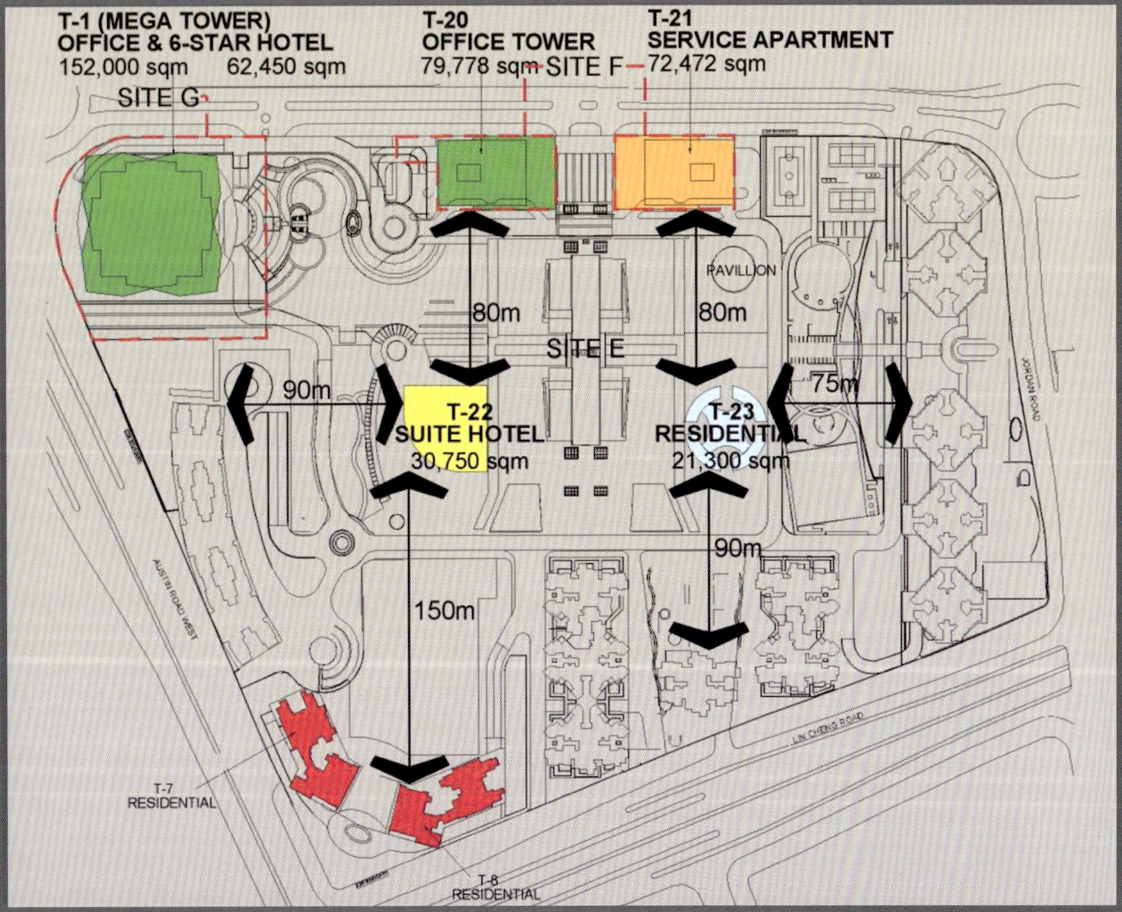

Left, above: KPF's proposed master plan highlights ICC in relation to West Kowloon's residences, luxury hotels and the outdoor plaza Civic Square at Union Square.

Left, below: One of the earlier versions of ICC took on a square floor plate positioned along a roughly east-west axis. It was part of a study to reduce the number of towers at Union Square by amalgamating office, hotel and residences.

Right, above: KPF's initial concept proposals for ICC included a 480 metre high building that was similar to an extruded square column, incorporating hotel and offices.

Right, below: Another version of KPF's initial proposal for ICC was a tapering tower that reached a height of 580 metres with a decorative spire capping its top.

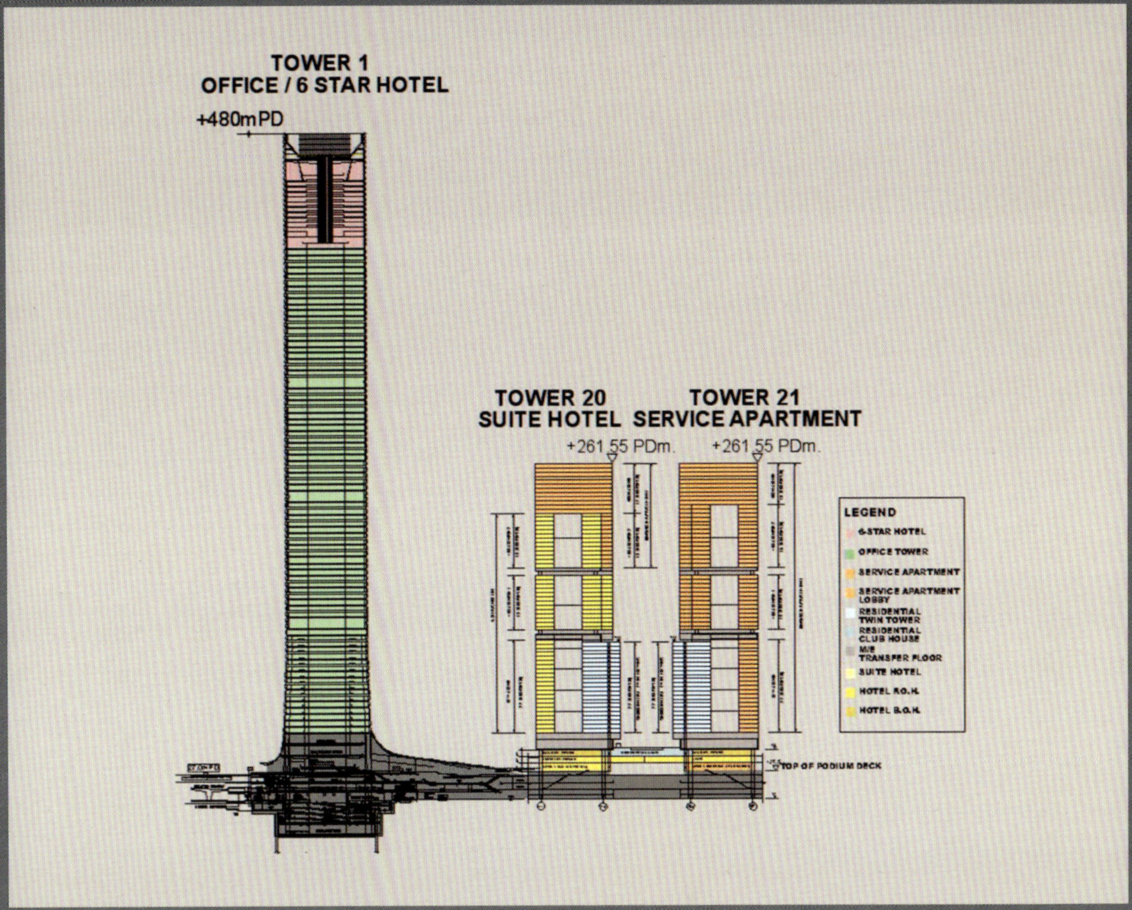

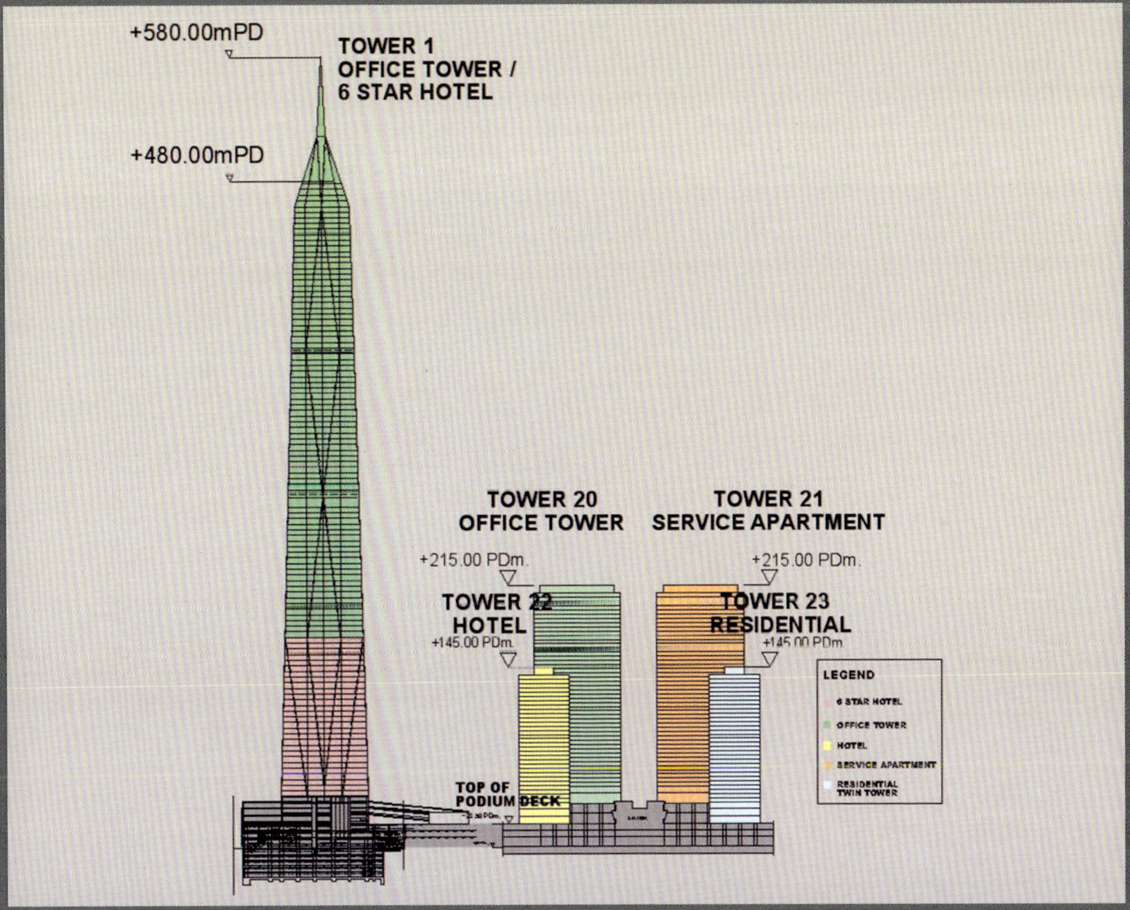

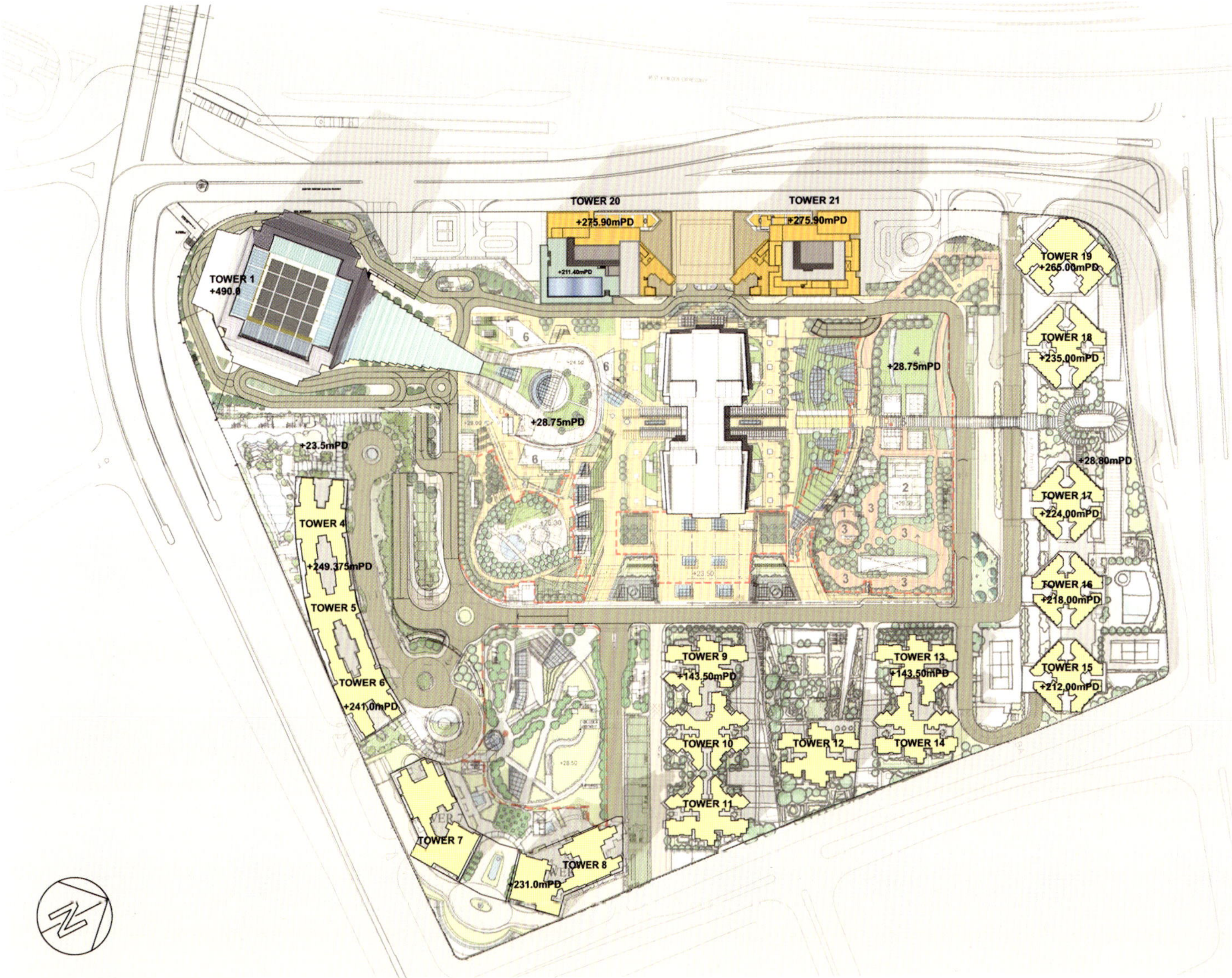

Opposite page: Wong & Ouyang's rendering of ICC against the Hong Kong skyline shows the building's notched corners and its mechanical floors in relation to the rest of the tenant occupied ones.

Above: A rendered plan shows ICC in relation to nearby residential buildings after their completion, as well as the many pockets of green spaces surrounding them.

Shanghai: The Bund to Pudong

With David Lung, former Dean and currently Lady Edith Kotewall Professor in the Built Environment, Faculty of Architecture, The University of Hong Kong

Shanghai earned its reputation as the Paris of the east with good reason. At the dawn of the 20th century, the head offices of China's major banking institutions stretched along the 1.5 kilometre western bank of the Huangpu River.

It was known as The Bund, a play on the Persian word for embankment. International trading houses and consulates gave the area a cosmopolitan feel underscored by it being part of the former Shanghai International Settlement. Glamorous nightclubs and luxury hotels supported the tycoons' extravagant lifestyles, and establishments such as the Shanghai and Masonic clubs provided comfortable havens where guests could speak easy.

Architecturally, The Bund is an eclectic collection of Neoclassical aesthetics that reflected this sophisticated image. A building boom in the late 19th and early 20th century resulted in stately buildings that ran the gamut from Gothic Revival to Beaux Arts, with an unparalleled collection of Art Deco structures. Yet due to their uniqueness, this series of buildings proved to be too precious to be torn down despite their unsuitability for today's central business district requirements. In the 1980s, the Central Government of Beijing designated Pudong, directly across from The Bund, as a new financial hub to be developed. Cranes began to dominate the skyline and the once agricultural land became known for its glass and steel skyline courtesy of some of the world's best architects.

David Lung, Lady Edith Kotewall Professor in the Built Environment at The University of Hong Kong's Faculty of Architecture, knows Shanghai intimately and has been visiting the city as a child as his family owned a pharmaceutical company there. "At that time, Hong Kong was known as a resort destination while Shanghai was a place to do business," he recalls. "Shanghai and Hong Kong started at more or less the same time in the 1840s. They were both cities under foreign influences, with different destinies. Hong Kong, particularly its architecture, has always been very monolithic and British. Our mode of thinking and way of understanding western culture is purely British. Shanghai, by contrast, was influenced by the French, Germans, Japanese, Russians and Americans. It is more cosmopolitan as a result."

"When I first visited Shanghai, I encountered elderly Chinese people speaking French," Lung remembers. "I stayed in the Jinjiang Hotel and couldn't plug in any of my electronics because they were using a European system. Waiters were dressed in white, serving steaks. It was very elegant, even right after the Cultural Revolution. People bowling in bowling alleys had their pins picked up by staff, just like the old days in Hong Kong Club. When Hong Kong got its first set of escalators in the 1960s, people lined up to use them. Shanghai had its first escalators in the 1930s."

As Shanghai's development ground to a halt from 1950 to 1980, it was able to keep its historic buildings. "Modern Shanghai understands the importance of combining a modern city with its deeply rooted cultural background," says Lung. "Xintiandi, for example, uses a historical theme to package the entire area. This is a leading trend in development. As both Hong Kong and Shanghai are commercial cities like New York, both were under pressure to develop. When I took part in a HKU academic exchange in the 1980s, Shanghai was already moving along in its architectural preservation efforts. Pudong started taking shape in the 1980s and attracted investors from

Hong Kong, who brought along their architects and engineers. What we see today has been carefully orchestrated between urban, municipal and economic planners. Shanghai is a modern city yet its culture has been retained. There are a lot of historic districts for ordinary people to enjoy."

It was never a question whether The Bund's look and feel was to be retained. "The Bund is Shanghai's signature—people have this in mind," explains Lung. "This strip had to be retained, and prices along it were so high that even HSBC couldn't buy back its former building. That was what drove the move to Pudong: land economics."

Meanwhile, there was talk before and after Hong Kong's handover that Hong Kong, Shenzhen and Macau would eventually become one large metro area—a super city. "Along with that scenario, the whole CBD would move north, with a centre in Mongkok or Prince Edward," says Lung. "Sun Hung Kai Properties is quite far sighted. ICC is a result of it anticipating what was going to happen in the future. Every developer wants to have large floor plates for its traders. How many sites in Central can give tenants that?"

Yet architectural considerations aside, how has Pudong fared as a true shift for Shanghai's CBD? Is it just a collection of shiny new buildings without a soul? Sophie Kalkreuth, an editor formerly based in Shanghai and Hong Kong, views Pudong's success with skepticism. "It's contrived," she acknowledges. "It's not a walkable district. There are some sidewalks but there is no reason to be a pedestrian in Pudong. All the residential developments are along the water but are gated compounds. Everyone who lives there has his own car and driver. If you live and work in Pudong, you don't ever have to leave."

The demographic makeup of Pudong tends to be families and older expatriates from western or other Asian countries. "It's rare to see younger people choosing to live in Pudong," she says. "While it's easier and cleaner than the other districts in Shanghai, it's also very expensive." She notes that some of the newer compounds are equipped with amenities such as gyms and pools, with one even having its own man made beach. There are also many spanking new shopping malls and international schools in the district to cater to the expats' families, yet the only large outdoor park is Pudong Century Park. And despite the massive boulevards, traffic is often congested, with the underground tunnel connection between Pudong and Puxi particularly bad.

"No one was excited when our office moved to Pudong," admits Kalkreuth.

3/

CONNECTING THE SPINE

Connectivity is one of the key components to ICC's design, and that connectivity has a direct correlation to how rail transportation has evolved in Hong Kong over the past century. In a vertical city with less than 8% of the population owning private vehicles, public transportation in the form of taxis, buses, rail and light rail is something taken for granted. More than 90% of Hong Kong residents depend on public transportation for their daily journeys—the highest rate of passengers in the world. Due to its efficiency and reliability, on the rare occasion when a train is delayed or breaks down, the event becomes a lead story in the evening news.

Hong Kong has long enjoyed a relationship with rail. To some, train travel was viewed as a romantic way to explore the Far East. Still others saw it as a practical means to transfer goods and livestock. Sometimes, those two visions co-exist side by side, as it was not uncommon for the same train to carry passengers and freight initially. When the Kowloon Canton Railway (KCR, merged with MTR in 2007) opened in 1910, its terminus at Tsim Sha Tsui soon became the destination for intrepid travellers who ventured across Europe and China. Except for the period from 1949 to 1979 when the China border was closed to British Hong Kong, rail was the primary means of exchange between the two territories.

Over time, villages and then towns began to spring up organically around rail stations. In the 1960s, Hong Kong's first planned community—its first new town—was developed near Sha Tin rail station. Though local businesses and services supported these new towns, Hong Kong's shift from manufacturing to a service-based economy meant that many people needed to commute to work. It made sense that they lived near a rail station, where access to transportation was more convenient. Despite much government and private sector effort to diversify business away from Hong Kong's city centre, though, Central is still where many people work today.

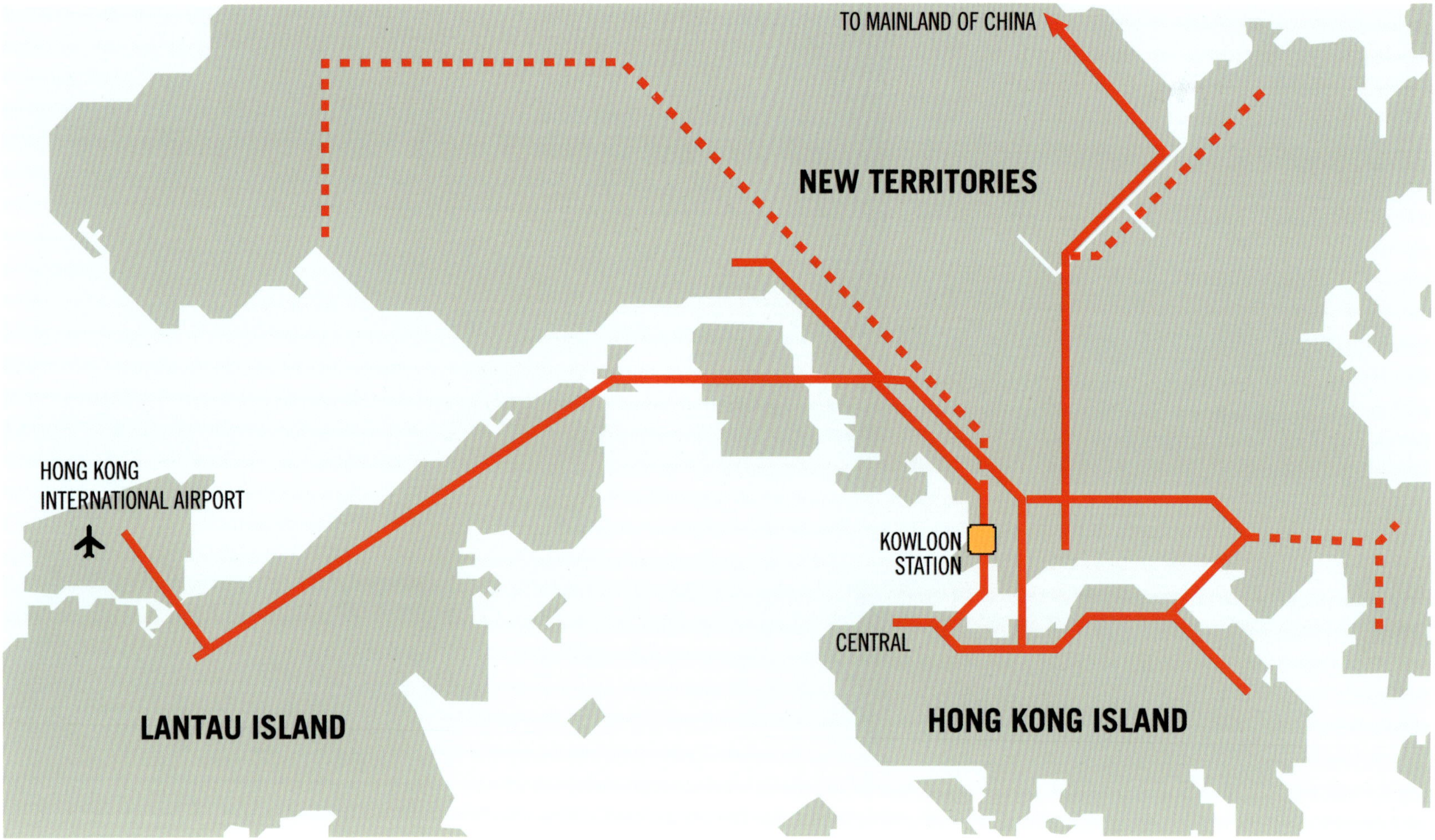

Fast forward to ICC's development. MTRC's master layout plan in 1995 for the top of Kowloon Station originally consisted of a 374 metre tower to comply with draft statutory height limits for the airport at Chek Lap Kok. The height was revised when the gazetted airport height restriction statutory limit was set at 580 metres. This allowed for a better design and structural form to overcome the area's geotechnical constraints. After Sun Hung Kai Properties won the development package in 2000, the tower height was further reduced to 490 metres after additional concept consideration.

"The original idea was to have a 580 metre iconic building," recalls Augustine T.S. Lee, architect and project director with Sun Hung Kai Properties. "We increased the gross floor area and reduced the height at the same time. It was a practical approach that emphasised the idea that ICC was not to be an ego-driven building."

Being located on top of a rail station gave ICC many advantages—a point taken by David Malott, principal with Kohn Pedersen Fox (KPF) and the design architect of ICC. "The connectivity of the building is its most important aspect," says Malott. "This building really shows how it plugs into a larger sustainable infrastructure. The Hong Kong government planned the airport relocation. Buildings would increase the density in locations where there are stations. Rail as an alternative to cars gives us an alternative to urban sprawl. It's a way of investing in the city's centre.

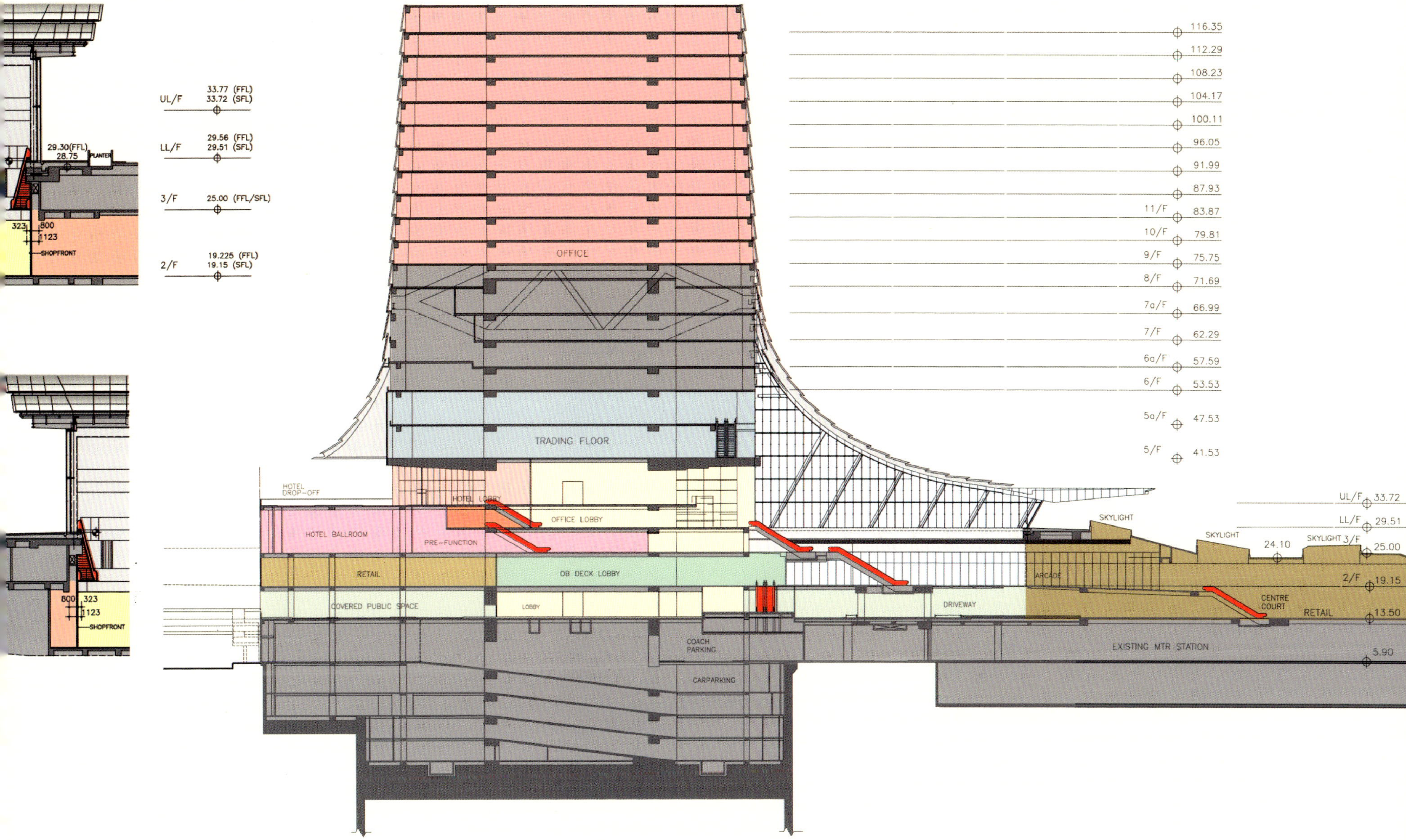

Opposite page: A simplified map of the various rail connections that link Hong Kong, Kowloon, the New Territories and the outlying island of Lantau where Hong Kong International Airport is situated. Kowloon Station is at the nexus of the city's rail grid.

Above: A section through the lower levels of ICC explains how parking, Kowloon station, retail, hotel, observation deck lobby and office lobby relate to each other within a tight footprint.

Below: In 2012, the site for the West Kowloon Terminus site of the Guangzhou Shenzhen Hong Kong Express Rail Link (XRL) can be glimpsed between the luxury residences adjacent to ICC.

Opposite page: The excavated XRL construction site in 2012. When completed in 2018, the XRL will further increase West Kowloon's connectivity to mainland China by cutting travel time between Hong Kong and Guangzhou to a mere 45 minutes.

Following pages: Central and Tsim Sha Tsui are serviced by a network of ferries that shuttle commuters and pleasure seekers to outlying island, Macau and a number of destinations along the Pearl River Delta.

COTAI STRIP

Discovery Bay

DiscoveryBay 1

Above: ICC is located near the Hong Kong China Ferry Terminal and cruise terminals located at Harbour City, making it a convenient destination for visitors arriving by sea.

Opposite page, left: ICC's proximity to arteries such as the Western Harbour Tunnel and Austin Road means that travelling to or from the building is quick and convenient.

Opposite page, right: Commuters heading home via the Western Harbour Tunnel in the evening are sometimes treated to colourful skies and sunsets.

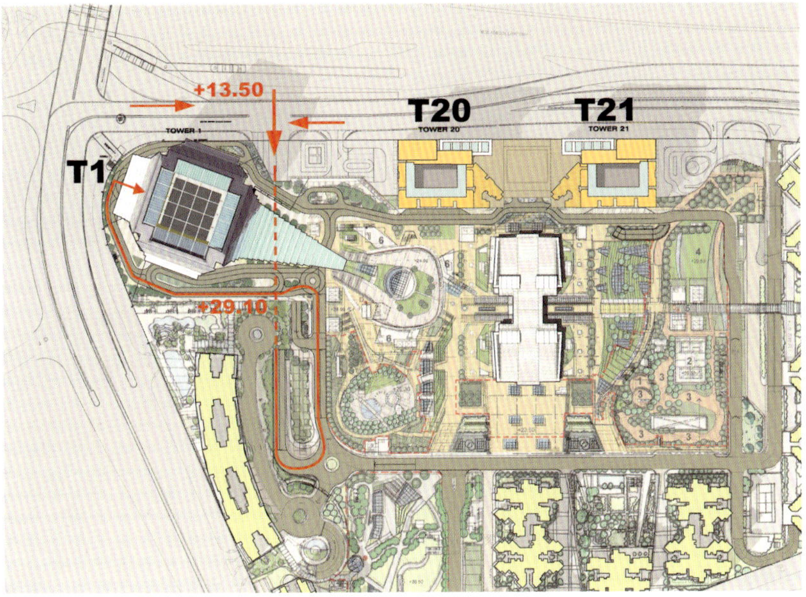

"Compared to other urban centres, Hong Kong's relationship between density and sustainability is one of the lowest of any city in the world. The climate works in Hong Kong's favour. People don't have to drive; they can walk from place to place. There are many ways to get to a destination. Hong Kong is one of the world's most interconnected cities, allowing for most of the territory to be preserved as greenery. It has set itself up for the next century by being so plugged in already."

"When connectivity improves, people are pulled together," notes Tony W.M. Tang, deputy project director with Sun Hung Kai Properties. "The best brains get pulled together to stimulate the entire development. You can look at ICC as a large capacity USB."

The connectivity that ICC enjoys is the result of careful planning. "How do you construct a tall building on a small site?" muses Artur C.K. Au-Yeung, director with Wong & Ouyang, ICC's project architect. "Normally, the site is much bigger for this type of building. Access is the second challenge. The typical building has ground floor access and a vast front court. People see the building and approach it. With ICC, many people approach it by car via a tunnel. How do we make this building's approach significant if we can't see it except from a distance?

"The other major challenge is ICC's number of occupants. There is 2.5 million square feet of office space plus a hotel. We have to cater for the number of vehicles visiting this building plus the people coming via public transport. One level of access is not enough. In the end, there are three levels for people and two levels for vehicles. Car drop off is on the ninth floor. And there is linage to MTR, the shopping arcade and everything else. The challenge was connecting the vertical with the horizontal."

"ICC is the last part of the Kowloon Station development," says Ernest C.M. Chan, chief structural engineer with Sun Hung Kai Architects and Engineers. "Everything else was already built, including a lot of expensive residences. We needed to consider the construction since we couldn't produce too much noise or work overnight. Our working hours were limited to 7am to 7pm. As we were building beside the MTR, we had to be very sensitive to their needs."

While Hong Kong Station and IFC in Central can be viewed as similar in scope to Kowloon Station and ICC, the Kowloon Station site is twice as large. Consequentially, it is developed as a mix use community with 6,000 housing units and supporting facilities. Hong Kong Station's developments are predominantly commercial—it does not have a residential component other than serviced apartments at Four Seasons Place.

ICC's connectivity card will get a further boost once the Guangzhou Shenzhen Hong Kong Express Rail Link (XRL) is completed in 2018 and the West Kowloon Terminus (WKT) is open. Located a short distance east of ICC, XRL will introduce another chapter to ICC's ever evolving connectivity, reducing the current travel time to Guangzhou by more than half on a dedicated new line.

"WKT is an important hub for mainland Chinese," says Margaret Chan. "It is the first and only stop in the city's core. XRL's speed will bring a completely different notion of transportation and distance to people. It only takes 45 minutes to get to Guangzhou; the world will seem so much smaller. When it opens, more people are willing to travel. It explains why so many mainland Chinese are investing in the Kowloon area: they are anticipating the completion of WKT. XRL will bring short and medium haul distance cities much closer to our reach and vice versa. Within an hour to three hour living circle, there is a huge catchment of people who will benefit from this intercity rail connection."

Above: The parking levels within ICC's basement are designed in a style that reiterates the elegance of the other public spaces within the complex.

Opposite page: A reflecting pond provides a sophisticated focal point between the underground entries to ICC and Elements shopping mall.

ICC

LOUIS VUITTON

Opposite page: A view of the Western Harbour Tunnel toll gate with ICC and the Hong Kong skyline beyond.

Above: From Victoria Harbour, ICC towers above the hills of Kowloon in the far distance.

Following pages: Construction continues on XRL's West Kowloon Terminus in 2014.

4/

SELECTING THE MASTER BUILDING

When Sun Hung Kai Properties won the project to build what eventually became ICC in September 2000, the Hong Kong developer knew even then that the building had to be special. At the time, Two IFC in Central was already well under construction and slated to be, for a brief time, Hong Kong's tallest building. By also constructing ICC across Victoria Harbour, Sun Hung Kai Properties was able to envision the two towers as a pair of icons that would physically and symbolically become the city's gateway to China. On a practical level, it could also learn lessons from IFC about what to do or avoid when it came to an even taller super skyscraper.

"We are a very practical company," says Tony W.M. Tang. "We asked several internationally renowned architects, including the architect who designed IFC, to compete for the design of ICC. In the end, KPF's proposal best fit our understanding and desire for a high rise commercial building in terms of structure and dynamics. It was a fast exercise: KPF was awarded the contract in December 2000 and we quickly started working with them to fine tune the design."

Unlike many of its counterparts that chose "starchitects" to make a statement through a singular building, Sun Hung Kai Properties was looking for a design that fused usable floor plates with poetry. The site was too constricted for any flourishes that took away from leasable square footage; architects who wanted to make just a statement building were not considered priority competitors. Instead, Sun Hung Kai Properties sought a like-minded talent well versed in designing tall buildings who understood what it takes to keep a half-kilometre building both impressive and stable. The building would be part of the iconic Hong Kong skyline while standing apart. It had to be well integrated into a network of other facilities at the base while meeting that base humanely. And it had to form one half of a gateway, complimenting a building across the harbour by another architect without being a carbon copy. All in all, a tall order in more ways than one.

The shortlisted firms all had proven track records for designing no nonsense structures that are good returns on investment and landmarks at the same time. The last thing that SHKP wanted was to over-design the tallest building in the city. In this day and age of compliance, frivolity was a luxury that even the city's leading developer couldn't afford. "The brief emphasised efficiencies," remembers David Malott. "ICC was designed for financial services tenants, so it had to be very efficient. It's pretty hard to deviate from a square plan when designing for banks.

"We knew that the building would form a gateway and had to balance Two IFC. We wanted them to share a feeling but be distinct buildings. They are like two lighthouses on either side of Victoria Harbour. The trunk of the building had to be straightforward, but the base was where we achieved something more unique. ICC seems to be lifting at the base to create a canopy and connection to its surroundings. It splays out and connects with the rest of the city.

"During the competition, we and the other three firms all adopted square floor plates after reading the brief. But we were the only ones who emphasised how the building touched the ground. The greatest design attention was placed there."

Originally, ICC was capped with a flowering crown that eventually became more abstracted. "We started with the square and thought about how to make it more interesting," says Malott. "Every move had to be rationalised. We thought about how to treat the corners and by carving them out, we created more corner offices. Wind load was also reduced on the building by softening and easing the corners.

"We discussed how to contour the silhouette of the building. As it flares out at the base, one of the options was to also flare out at the top. If we flare it out, the tower can be shorter. But with a hotel at the top, it didn't make sense since the flared part of the building would be most susceptible to wind. Instead, we designed a smaller floor plate for the upper hotel floors, with planar elements that lifted up from the top and a flowering dematerialisation at the crown. It was a rational approach to building—and then we thought about how to make it poetic."

"On December 16, 2000, the selected architectural firms gave a big presentation," recalls Kenneth K.F. Mo, structural engineer and general manager with Sanfield, a division of Sun Hung Kai Properties. "The Kwok family (and board members of Sun Hung Kai Properties) took a look at KPF's design and said that it looked good." Awarding the design contract to KPF was a decision that took mere minutes, as it was immediately apparent to everyone present that KPF was able to meet—and actually surpass—all the aspirations the developer had for its landmark property in West Kowloon.

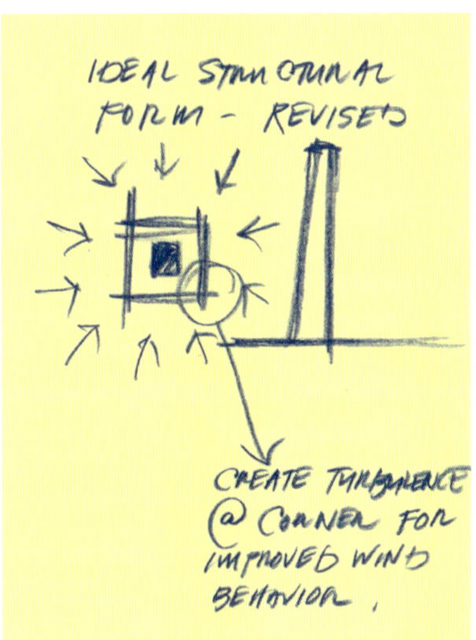

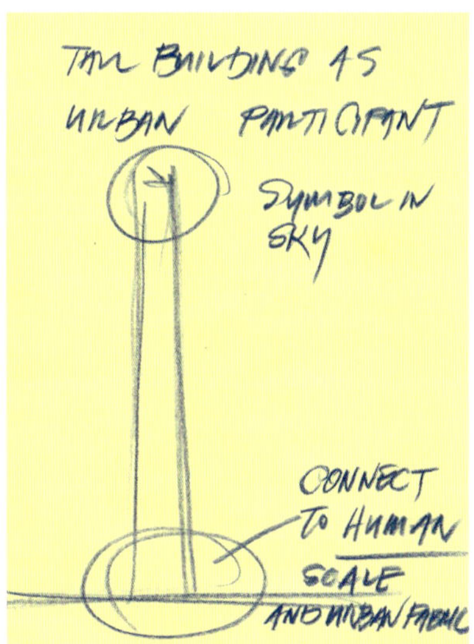

Top: The southwest and southeast facades split at the very top of ICC, affording a view of Central's skyline from the roof.

Above, left & right: KPF's preliminary sketch for what would eventually be ICC's final structural form; KPF understood from the outset that ICC was to be more than another office tower, as this sketch indicated that the firm envisioned the building to become both an urban participant as well as relate to human scale.

Opposite page: As ICC meets the ground, its facade begins to gently taper to a quartet of sheltering rooflines with the one extending outwards into an exaggerated train of glass scales.

Following pages: A view from Victoria Peak shows the two towers of 2IFC and ICC silently standing guard over the city.

Above: Streaks of light across the water follow the passing of ships; their dynamic brilliance is contrasted against the white lights that clad ICC's exterior.

Opposite page: ICC's external lighting programme transforms it into a column of illumination against the brilliant night sky of Kowloon.

Following pages: The contrast of skyscrapers and rolling hills take on a special glow at twilight as more and more lights twinkle on.

Paris: Ile-de-France to La Defense

With Valerie Portefaix, co-founder, MAP Office
and lecturer, Master of Design, School of Design,
Hong Kong Polytechnic University

On a sunny September Sunday, Paris is at its most charming. On such a day, standing at the outdoor viewing platform on the Eiffel Tower, a series of skyscrapers can be seen in the distance that seem incongruous with the rest of the city's homogenous, mostly low rise cityscape.

With its 3rd century B.C. origins as a settlement along the Seine River, Paris has indisputably been one of the world's cultural centres for centuries. Within its 20 arrondissements, or districts, rational city planning combined with lively street life give character and distinction to every corner. Years of strict adherence produced a skyline that is uniform in architectural scale and choice of materials broken by iconic monuments and urban parks, for a town-like ambience that is easily accessible.

Yet the past century has seen Paris become a financial hub for Europe, and the need for the larger floor plates and technological advances of modern high rise buildings became pressing. In the mid 1950s, what became Europe's largest purpose built business district came into being with La Defense. Named after the 1883 statue that commemorates soldiers who defended their city in the Franco-Prussian War, La Defense is sometimes regarded as the 21st arrondissement though it is actually located in the boroughs of Nanterre, Puteaux and Courbevoie.

La Defense is situated along a 10 kilometre line that begins at the Louvre and continues to the Arc de Triomphe. From the Grande Arche de la Defense, the path is clearly delineated with monumental structures forming anchors that link the old with the new. Due to planning principles outlined in the 1933 Athens Charter separating living and working spaces as well as vehicular and pedestrian linkages, La Defense was intended to be strictly a financial hub. The district replaced a number of slums, with its esplanade extending westwards from the Grande Arche showcasing some of the country's tallest skyscrapers. The first to be erected was the 1962 Esso building, replaced in 2001 by Coeur Defense by architect Jean-Paul Viguier. Building plans were stalled until the early 1970s when the RER, Paris' regional express network train system, was extended to connect La Defense with the city centre. Development then progressed in phases, with expansion in the mid 1990s that continues until today.

Valerie Portefaix, architect, co-founder of Hong Kong-based urban artists MAP Office and lecturer in the Master of Design programme at Hong Kong Polytechnic's School of Design, first visited La Defense out of curiosity more than two decades ago. Originally from Saint-Etienne in east central France, she went there with her partner Laurent Gutierrez and was less than impressed. "It is not a place that you return to," Portefaix states. "It's only for business. It is generally regarded as a failure. The podium underneath the Grande Arche is always windy and a space where everyone catches cold. It has a bad reputation."

"Parisian commerce is medieval," Portefaix believes. "Many entrepreneurs are like Wing Lok Street guys selling dried fish. La Defense came about due to the post World War II reconstruction. But the economy in France at the time was primarily industrial, with strong individual cities and strength in agriculture. La Defense is processional—very French. There is a concentration of development in a small area, and then transport to get to it but fusion of the development with others is avoided. La Defense is plugged into everything around it, but not really part of it."

Florent Maire, an executive with JPMorgan Chase in Hong Kong, previously worked in La Defense when he was an intern at Credit Agricole. Although he liked the open, minimal spaces of his office along the Esplanade, he bemoaned the lack of activities in the district. "There is nothing to do there," he says. "It lacks people and humanity. I never really walked around on the streets; it was very gusty and empty, with the sound of wind whistling through. It's not convenient to drive there and we entertained back in the city. By 7:30 pm, there wasn't anyone left—and it was unsafe at night with the reputation of gangs gathering there once it gets dark. The towns nearby are not nice places." Being surrounded by some of the poorer suburbs of Paris and with businesses that shut down when the sun sets has transformed La Defense into somewhat of an urban ghetto similar to American inner cities. Maire notes that some larger companies are seeking other options that are less expensive and further away from the city centre.

"When it was first launched, there were a lot of projects going on there," Portefaix recalls. "Many buildings were built very quickly, and they are not used to building things on that scale in France. The human ingredient was missing in the end."

She cautions against West Kowloon heading in the same direction. "In Hong Kong, West Kowloon is an obvious mirror response to Central. The city is famous for its combination of density and geography. There is strong urbanity in Central surrounded by green hills that's linked with the city's identity and history. West Kowloon still feels like you're walking on manmade land; like La Defense, it's an island. What's wonderful about Hong Kong is the mix of old and new."

Portefaix compares ICC and IFC to two lighthouses that together form a gate to the city. "The light catches the building in interesting ways at different times of the day," she says. "The façade is magical, like a fabric that is always changing. I think the district will make more sense when the cultural venues at West Kowloon Cultural District are completed."

5/
ICC

DESIGNING THE DRAGON

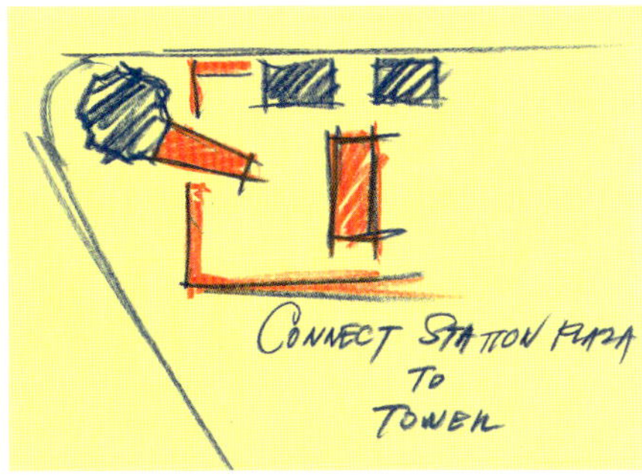

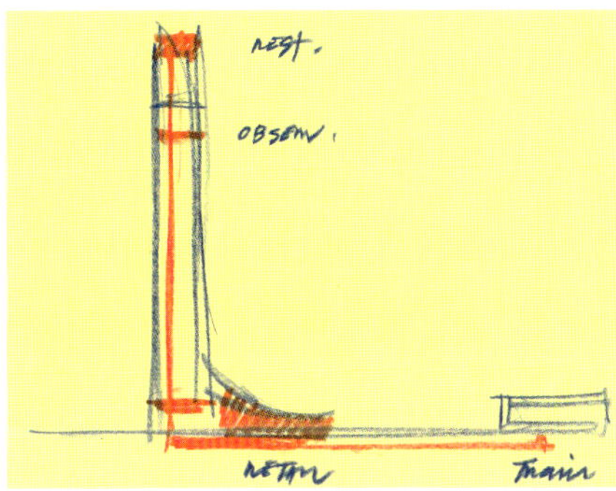

Sun Hung Kai Properties knew when it won the contract to develop ICC that it was not going to be just another tall building. First, its strategic location at the base of West Kowloon opposite Central meant that it was going to be a significant part of the Hong Kong skyline from two significant vantage points: upon approaching the city centre from the Hong Kong International Airport and from north Hong Kong island. It is one of those rare buildings that has no front, side or back, as it sits elevated on a podium surrounded by structures less than half its height. Like sculpture, it was to be seen in the round. The lack of a front façade meeting the street was one of the major challenges faced by KPF and Sun Hung Kai Properties. It led to KPF's development of the dragon's tail, arguably ICC's most stunning design feature. KPF envisioned the tail as a way to bring heaven down to earth to show people how to enjoy a tall building.

"ICC is one of the most complex buildings in the world in terms of end users," believes Augustine I.S. Lee, referring to its mixture of hotel, public observation floor dubbed Sky100, restaurant floor, offices and retail. "It is comparable to Shanghai World Financial Centre—also known as the bottle opener building—but that base is more sprawled. ICC's physical constraint is so significant. It has virtually no entrance from the street level.

"When we designed ICC, one of the biggest concerns was how people experienced the drive from the elevated row to the podium. It's a long drive through a tunnel—the drive itself becomes part of the experience."

After winning the competition in 2000, KPF refined its design for the dragon's tail. It was positioned towards Civic Square, an outdoor piazza connected to Elements shopping mall that boasts mid to upper mid end restaurants and bars facing an open central courtyard. "Civic Square is the plaza equivalent," says David Malott, referring to

Left, top: The entrance to ICC from within Elements shopping mall sits underneath a soaring canopy of glass shingles with clerestory to either side of it.

Left, bottom: KPF's structural study model of the dragon's tail as it touches down, showing how it relates to the proportions of people who will be using the space.

Opposite page: A view of ICC's notched corner in the higher part of the building allows a glimpse into the tenant's space within through the glass shingle cladding.

traditional tall buildings that met the street with a public plaza at its base. "The building curves down to engage that."

The tail consists of a series of vertical shingles that transition to a horizontal plane as it spreads out into a glass canopy closer to ground level; the canopy acts as a porte cochere for visitors arriving by car. From within Elements, the tail acts as a sweeping skylight that opens up as people approach ICC's tower. Each layer of shingles resembles abstracted dragon scales, underscoring the design theme. "The dragon's tail is directed at two stations: Kowloon Airport Express and Kowloon MTR on the Tung Chung line," says Lee. "It provides a good symbolic connection and spatial experience."

"The shingles scale down the building to make it brighter and lighter," notes Malott. "They break up the tall tower into more tangible human scale elements. One shingle is essentially one floor; that unit gets built up and repeated, to help understand the scale of the tower. Lower down on the building, the shingles open up and you can see gaps in between them. It feels like the building is breathing. The impact is light at the base, as if the building floats down barely scraping against the ground. It feels pleasant and friendly, not like a giant 490 metre tower."

"The shingles also afforded better weather protection, like roof tiles overlaying one atop another," adds Lee. "It acts like a sun shading device, with the overhang shielding off harsh daylight. And, as one layer of shingles is independent of another and not stacked, it is easy to change the inter floor arrangement."

Above, left: Another view of KPF's dragon tail model. As it descends, the tail would be secured by angled columns and rods. Scaled figures show the proportions of human in relation to the building's interior height.

Above, right: KPF's model showing a partial section of the dragon tail's scales as it meets an exterior glazed wall.

Opposite page, right: A typical office floor plan in ICC shows how angling the building roughly 45 degrees to the grid allows for views across the harbour to be maximised along three directions.

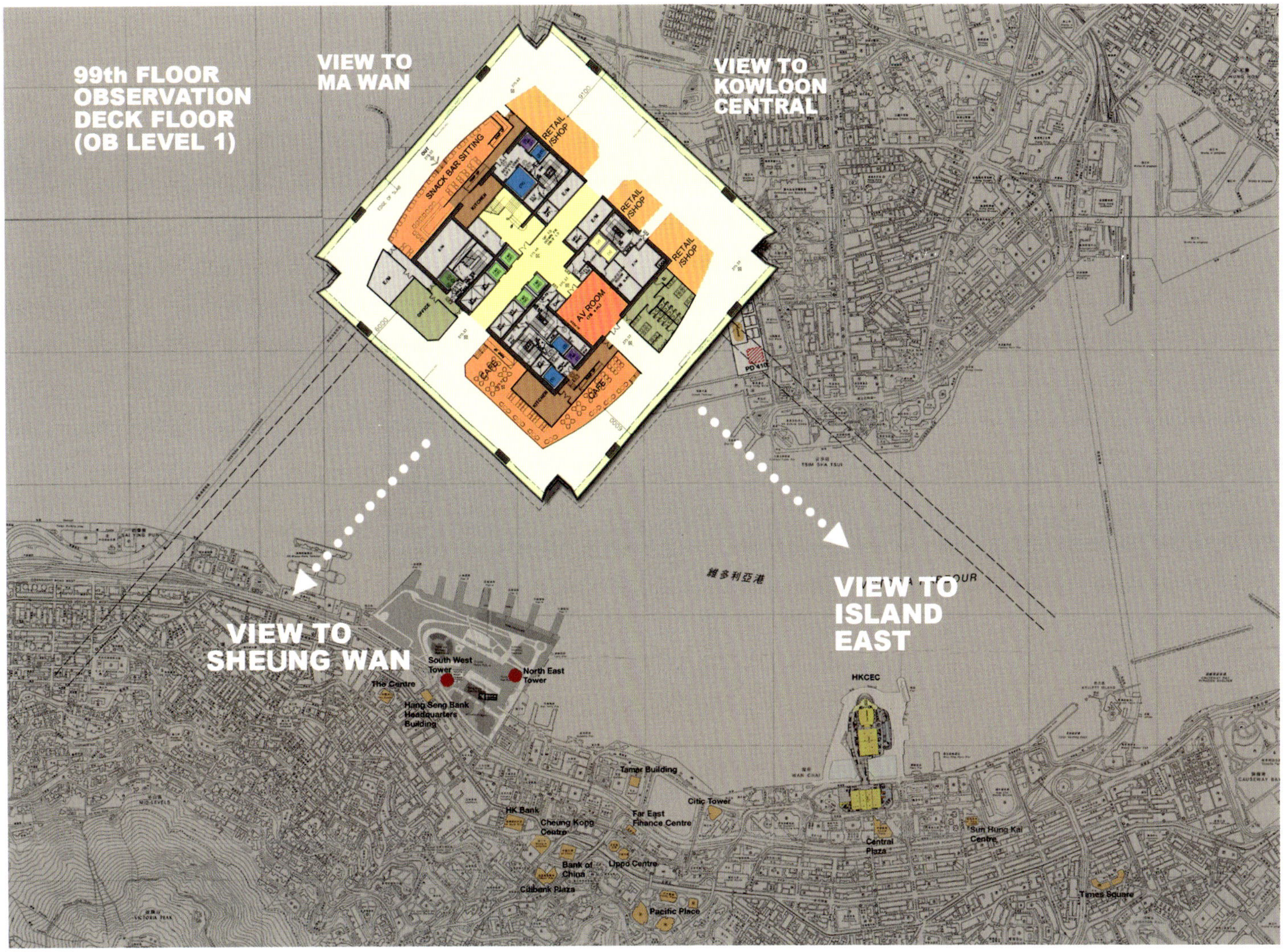

"A normal curtain wall has stacked components," says Malott. "At ICC, we could work on any part of the façade at any time and not interfere with the system. The shingles provided no obstruction to the views and reinforces the premise that this building is sitting above water."

"The slanted shingles on the façade contributed to reducing glare," says Artur Au-Yeung. "We used the same glass on the façade and the dragon's tail. As the side that faces Victoria Harbour offers the best views, we deepened the curtain wall to core dimension on that side."

One of the major changes that occurred during design development was the reorientation of a bank of lifts due to the shifting of the dragon's tail. As they provide the shuttle lifts to ICC's sky lobby, they were rotated to face passengers as they came up the escalators from the mall underneath the tail. "We spent a lot of time making the lobby work," recalls Lee. "There are five office zones plus The Ritz-Carlton, Hong Kong and sky100. We had to properly organise traffic at the entrance level."

For the offices, KPF kept floors open and flexible so that they could easily cater to individual tenants' specific requirements. "The typical office had eight columns per floor with expansive panoramic views," says Malott. Each floor plate allowed for eight corner offices due to the large size of ICC's corner cut outs.

D

Lee and Malott spent countless number of hours personally hand selecting the materials for ICC from around the globe to ensure that they reinforced their vision for the tower. "We came up with two main stones," says Mallott. "Roman travertine on the vertical faces of the core and green granite for the mega columns. We wanted a unique signature stone for the tower."

"The columns are huge and impressive," says Lee. "Verde Marina is the same stone that Steve Jobs wanted to use for his Apple store in Shanghai."

Backlit onyx from Iran was selected for the lobby, as it is a symbol for international commerce. Chandeliers were from the Czech Republic, stone flooring was from Brazil and titanium was from the United States. "Sun Hung Kai Properties was active about using a warm material palette," says Mallott. "It didn't want the building to feel too corporate. A lot of the interior profiles are curved to give a feeling of softness.

"We designed ICC to have a lifespan of 100 years. But of course we can't be living the same way as 100 years from now. We had to make sure what we're building is as relevant as possible, and can adapt its use well into the future. We had to resist the temptation of doing anything too flashy."

"The flexibility for development is a very important component to ICC," says Lee. "We are constantly improving the building to be relevant to the present while ensuring that there is future business."

"ICC has met or exceeded our expectations," states Malott. "We never imagined it to be this successful."

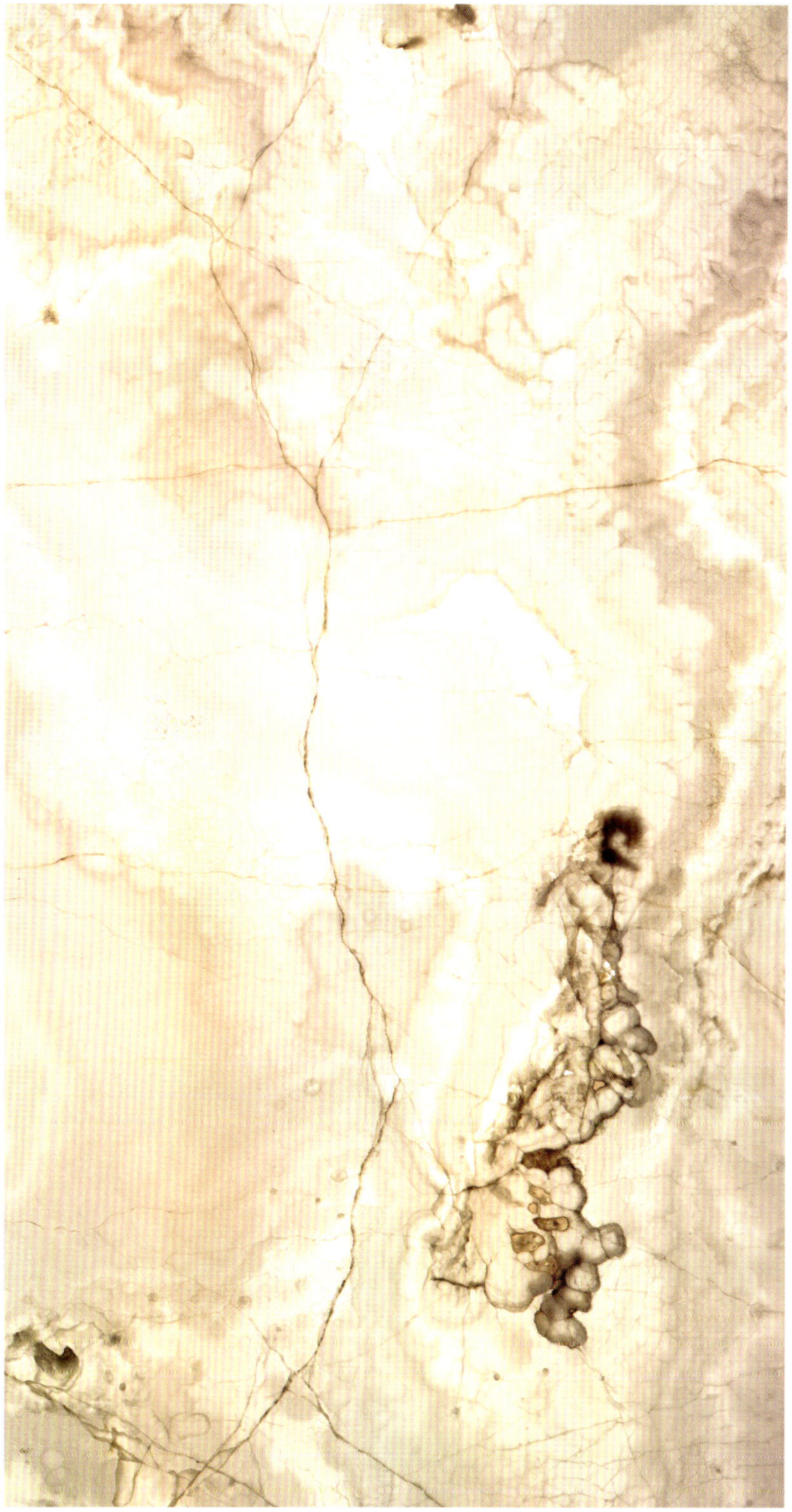

Opposite page: ICC is a grade A tower designed with top quality materials; the lift cabs are trimmed with bronze and large swaths of Roman travertine on walls.

Above: Elegant backlit onyx was selected for the ICC's lobby areas.

Above: One of the features of ICC that made it enticing to high profile international tenants was that it offered private concierge and entries for a few of its anchor tenants.

Left: A green wall of young bamboo provides a pleasant view from one of ICC's lobbies.

Opposite page, top: Large horizontal panels of bevel edged Roman travertine give the lobby a stately ambience.

Opposite page, bottom left: Ceiling bulkheads finished in timber add warmth to the public areas of ICC.

Opposite page, bottom right: To give definition to lobby volumes, Wong & Ouyang installed chandeliers that were akin to mobile art.

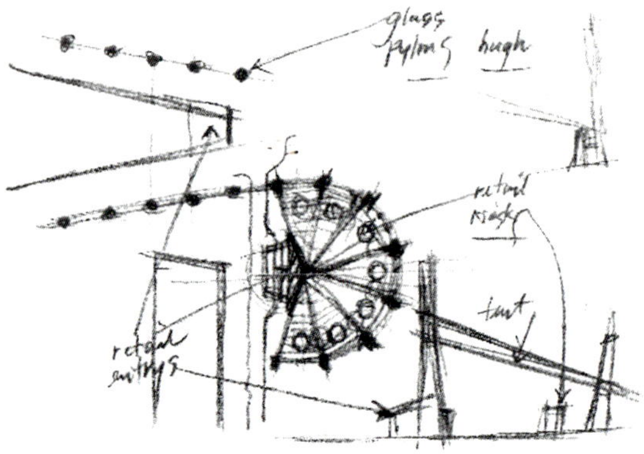

Left: Preliminary drawings by KPF in the year 2000 indicate how ICC would relate to its surrounding buildings at West Kowloon, as well as the initial development of the dragon's tail.

Above: One of KPF's later models of ICC and the resolution of the dragon's tail.

Opposite page: KPF's concept for ICC illustrates how the top and bottom of the building are graceful flourishes to an otherwise very efficient structure.

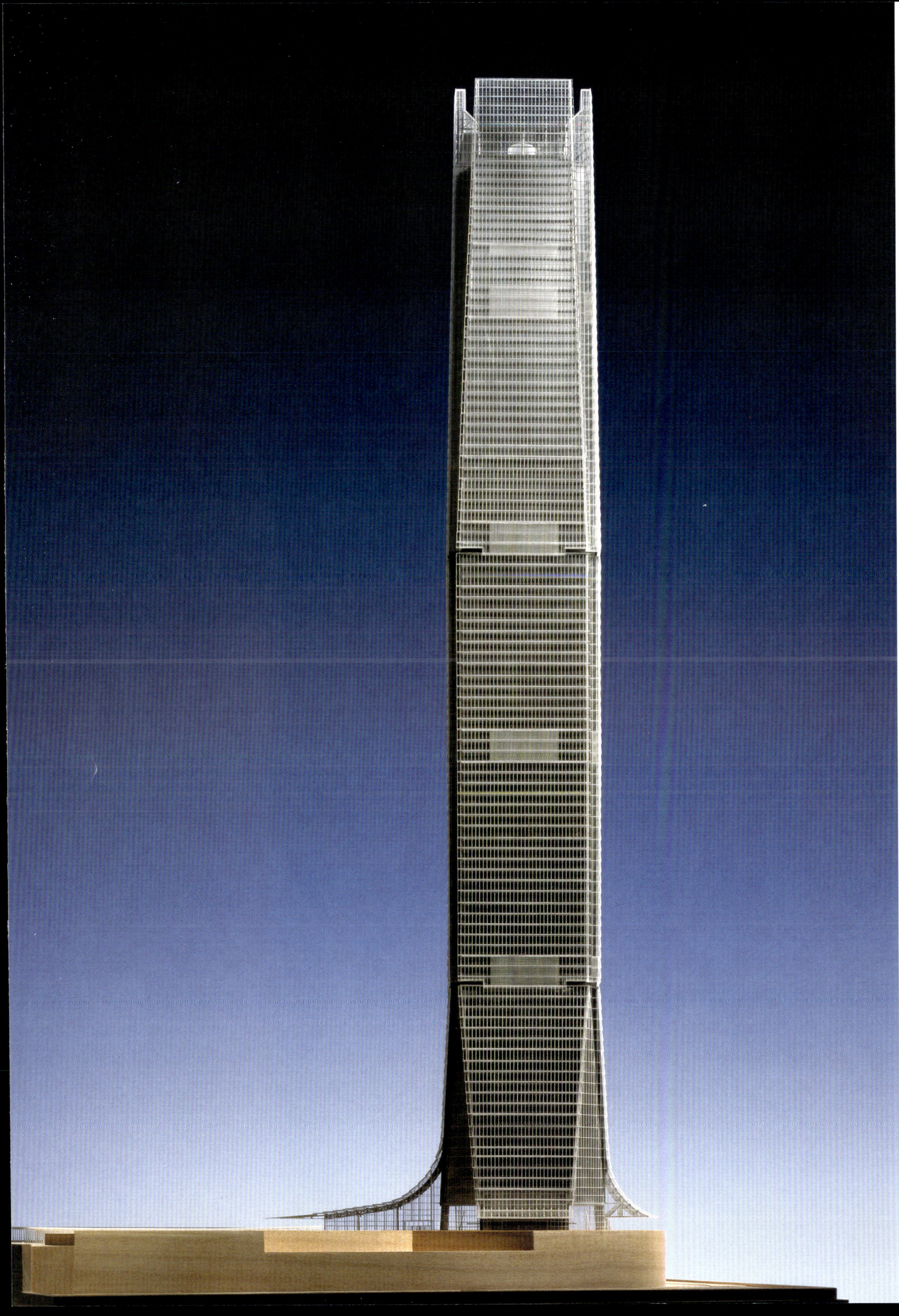

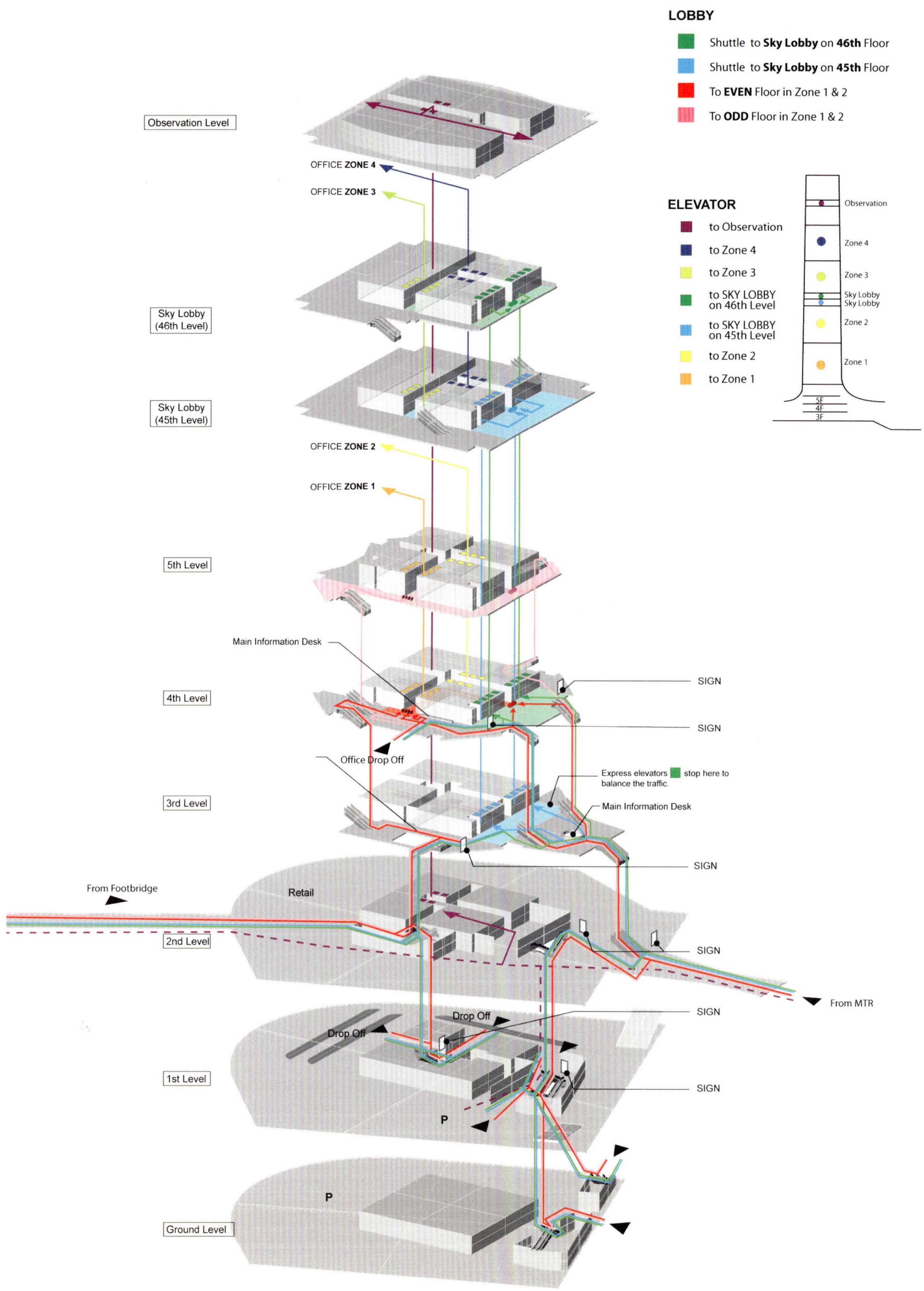
LOBBY
Shuttle to Sky Lobby on 46th Floor
Shuttle to Sky Lobby on 45th Floor
To EVEN Floor in Zone 1 & 2
To ODD Floor in Zone 1 & 2
ELEVATOR
to Observation
to Zone 4
to Zone 3
to SKY LOBBY on 46th Level
to SKY LOBBY on 45th Level
to Zone 2
to Zone 1
Observation
Zone 4
Zone 3
Sky Lobby
Sky Lobby
Zone 2
Zone 1
5F
4F
3F
Observation Level
OFFICE ZONE 4
OFFICE ZONE 3
Sky Lobby (46th Level)
Sky Lobby (45th Level)
OFFICE ZONE 2
OFFICE ZONE 1
5th Level
Main Information Desk
4th Level
SIGN
SIGN
Office Drop Off
Express elevators stop here to balance the traffic.
Main Information Desk
3rd Level
SIGN
From Footbridge
Retail
2nd Level
SIGN
From MTR
SIGN
Drop Off
Drop Off
1st Level
SIGN
P
P
Ground Level

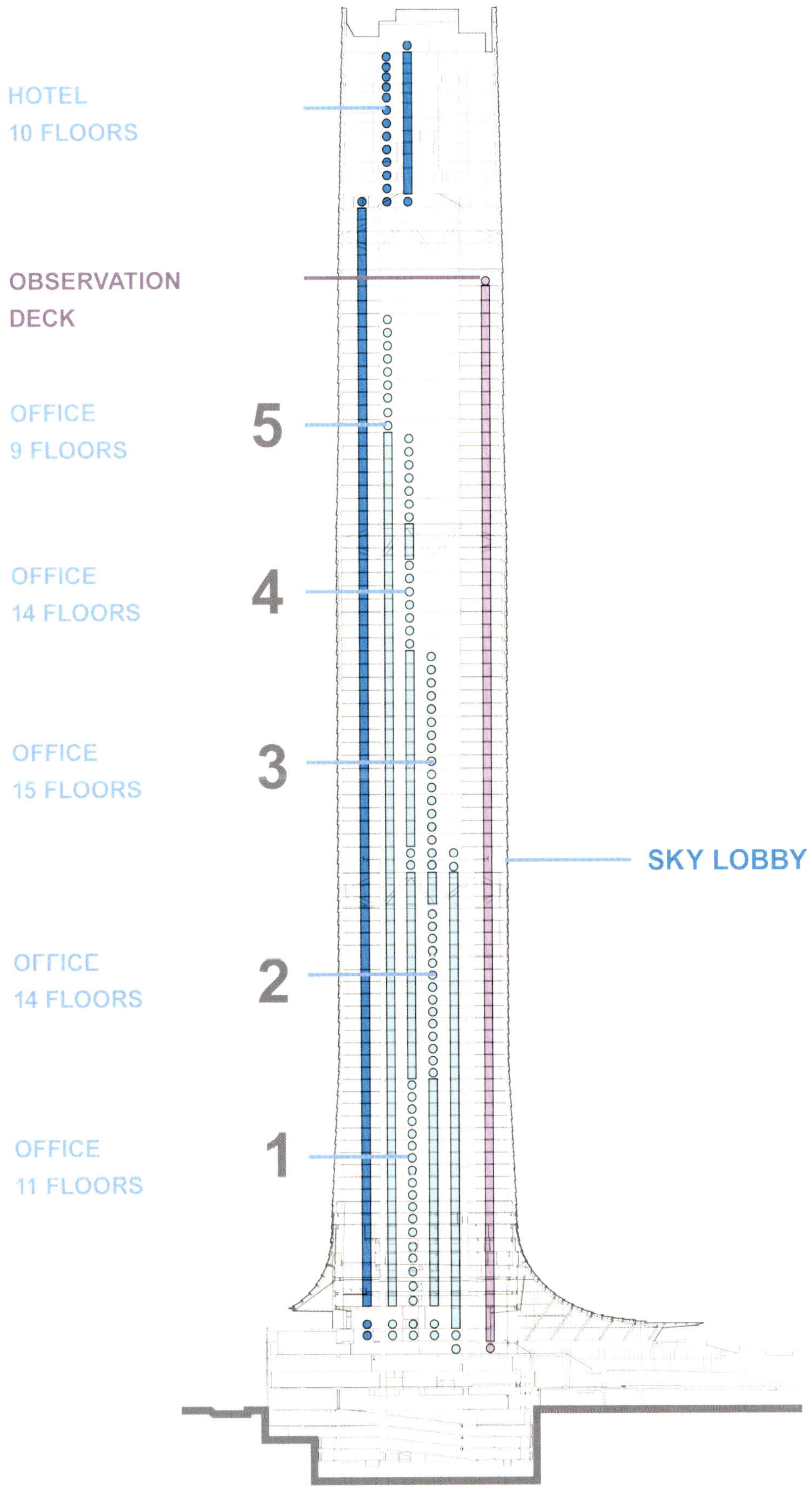

Opposite page: A stacking diagram shows how the key floors within ICC are laid out and related to each other vertically.

Left: The various lifts that services different zones in ICC is indicated by a colour-coded section.

Shuttle lift arrangement

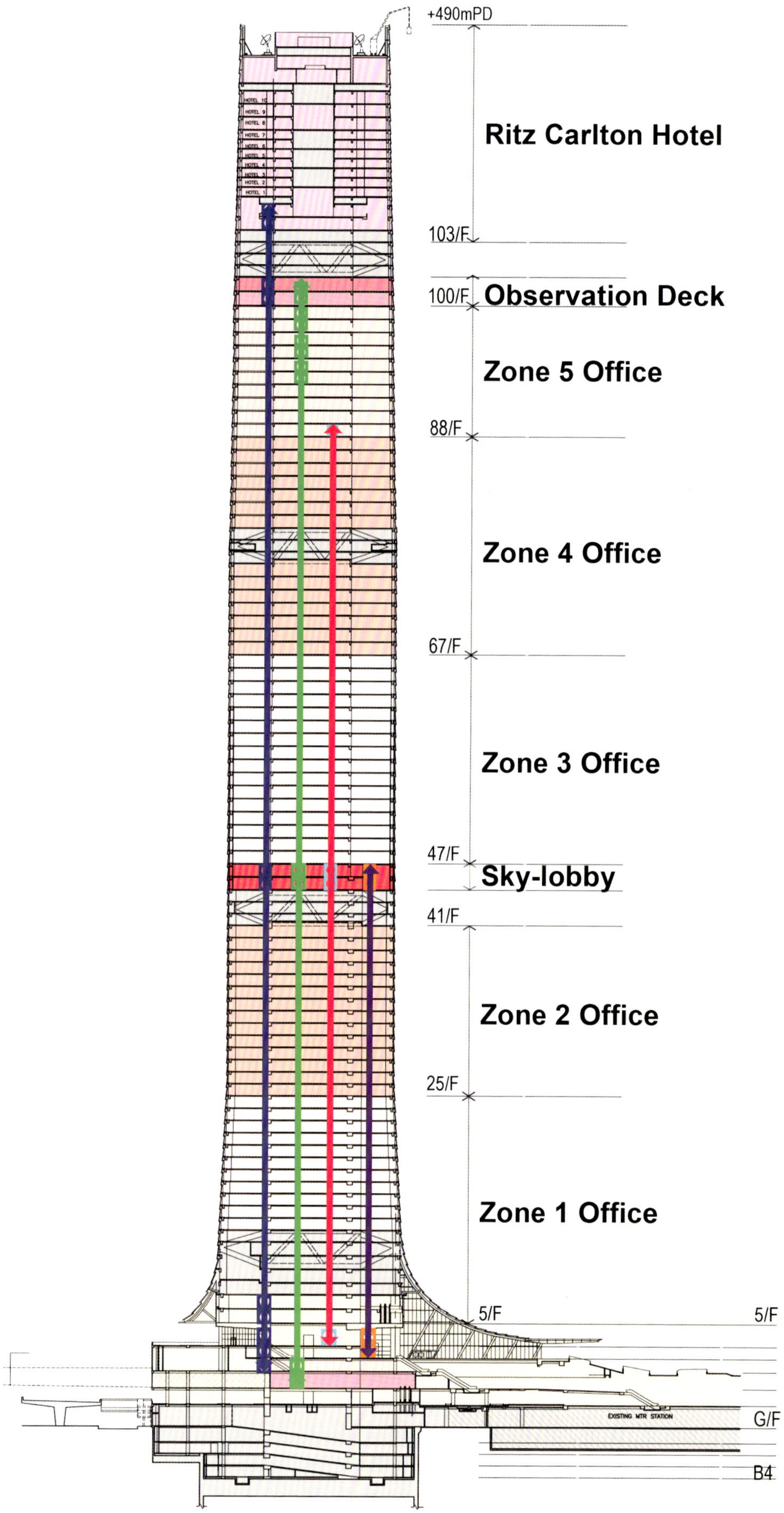

Right: A section through ICC highlights the different types of tenants occupying the building, and the sky lobbies that service them.

Opposite page: Two floor plans of ICC explain how the office lobby is positioned relative to the hotel lobby.

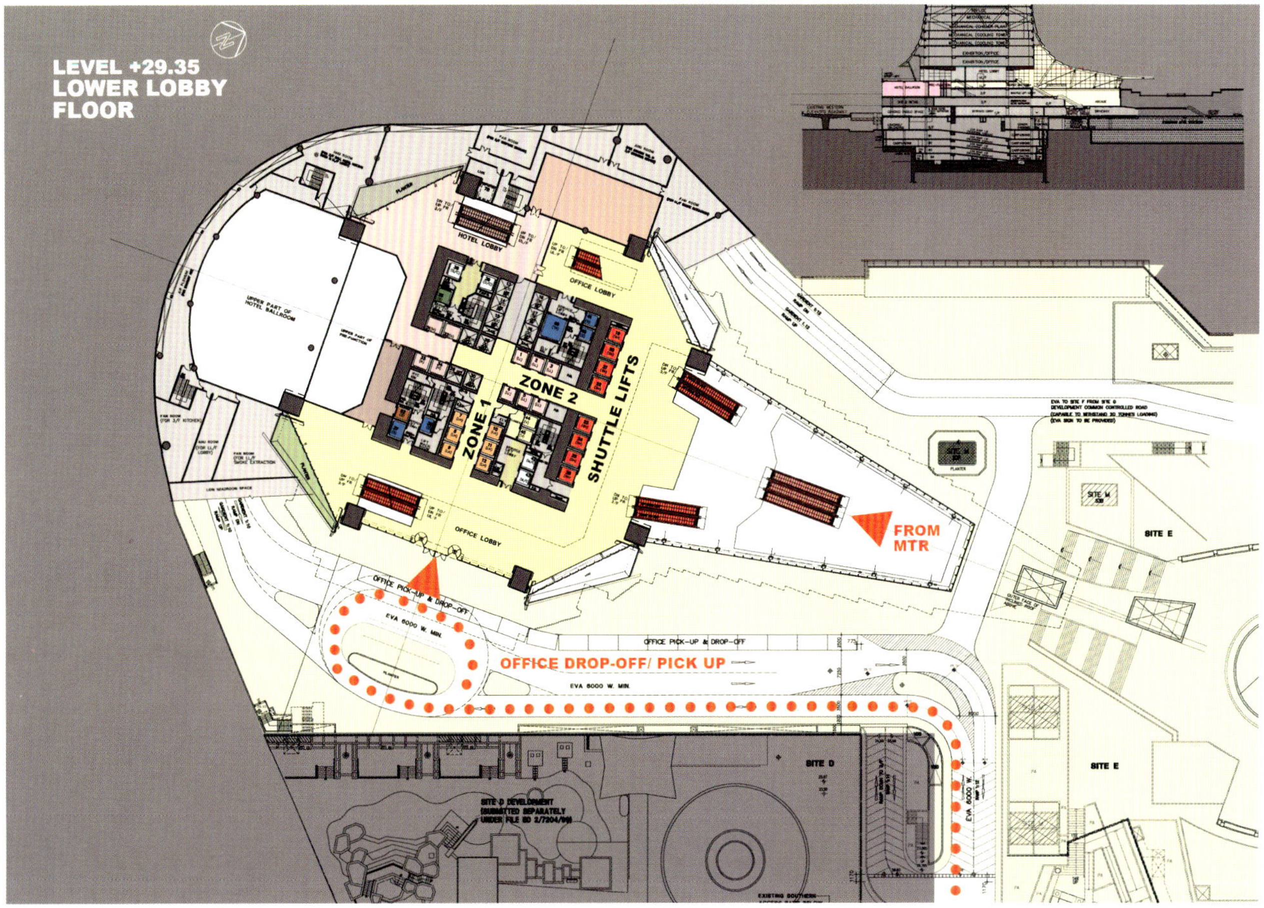
LEVEL +29.35
LOWER LOBBY
FLOOR
ZONE 1
ZONE 2
SHUTTLE LIFTS
FROM
MTR
OFFICE DROP-OFF/ PICK UP

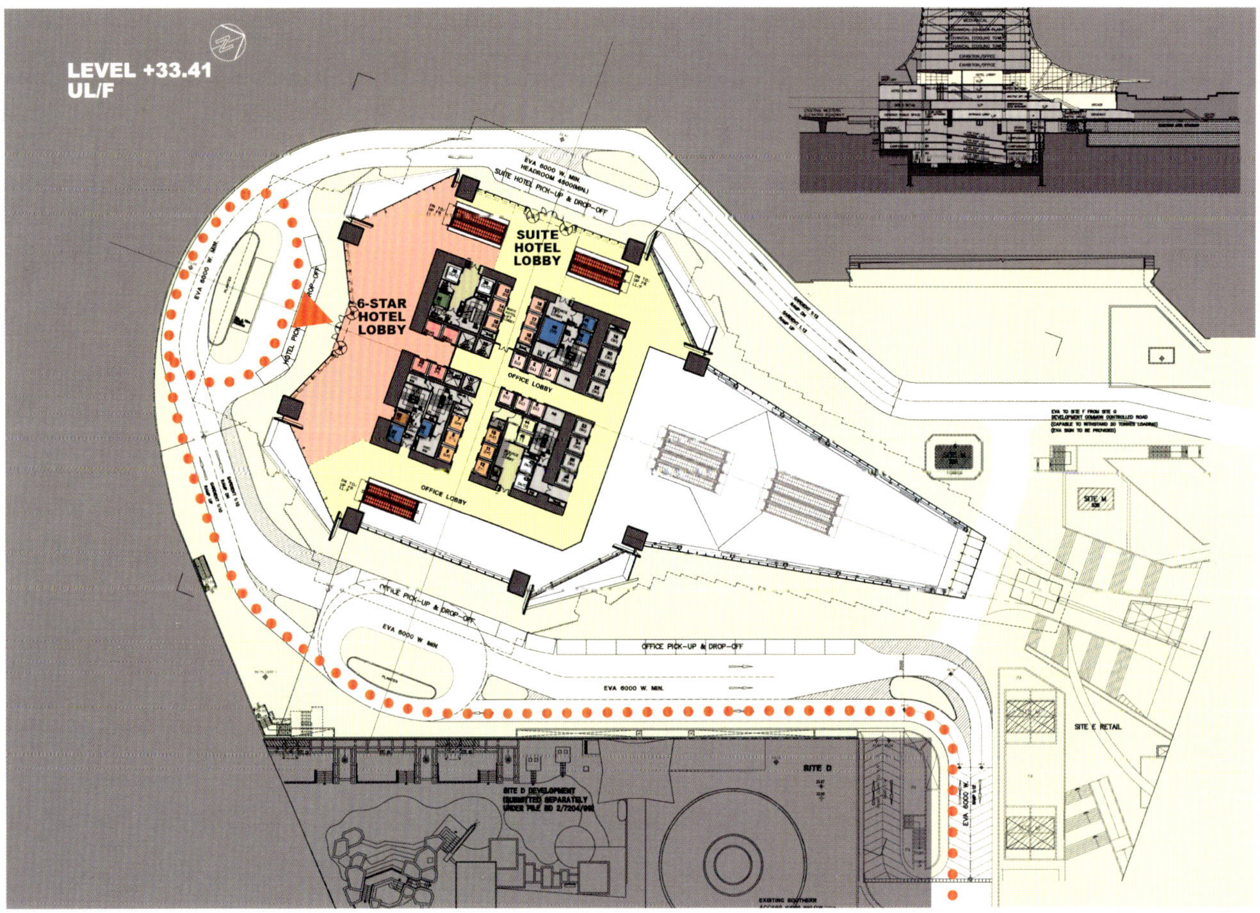
LEVEL +33.41
UL/F
SUITE
HOTEL
LOBBY
6-STAR
HOTEL
LOBBY

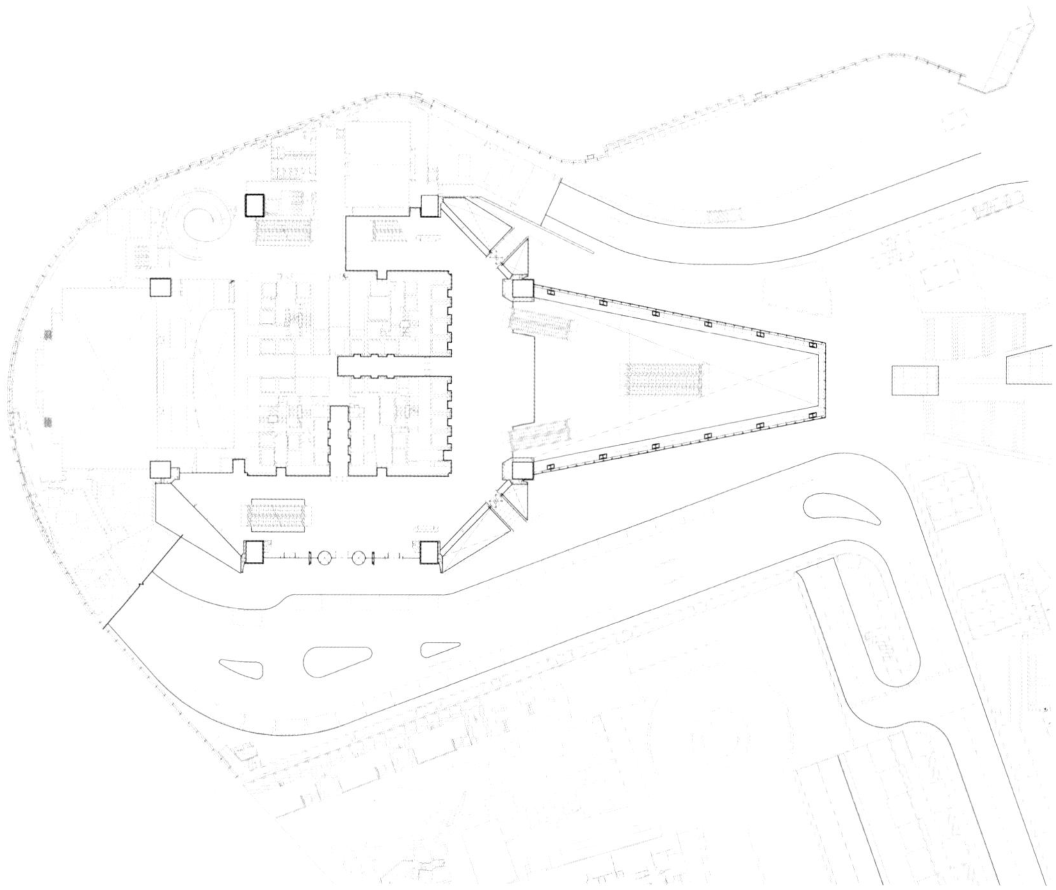

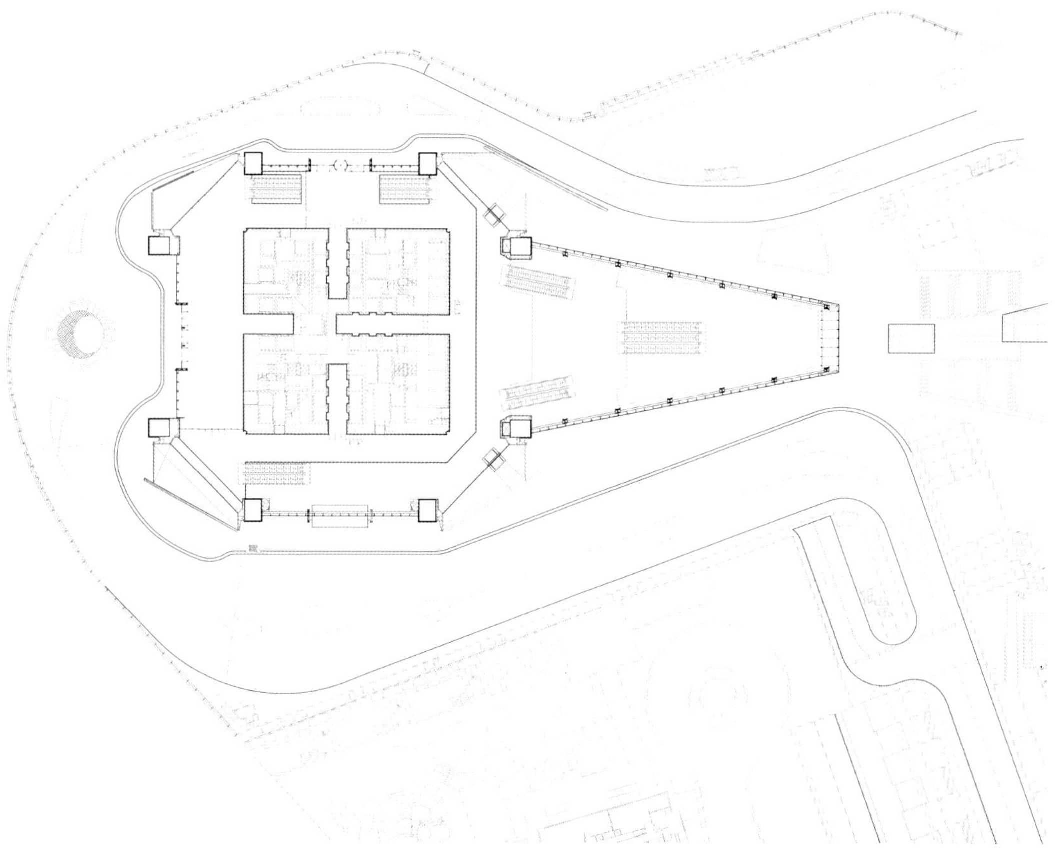

Right, above and below: Site plans of ICC at different heights show how the core differs at podium level compared to a higher level after the tower rises away from the podium, and the different drop off points on each floor.

Opposite page: Six floor plans of ICC reveal (clockwise from top left) a typical lower level office configuration; sky100, a lower level floor in The Ritz-Carlton, Hong Kong; a higher level floor in The Ritz-Carlton, Hong Kong; a typical higher level office configuration; and the reception floor for The Ritz-Carlton, Hong Kong.

Following pages: ICC's shingles dramatically transitions from vertical to horizontal as it tapers into a long tail, with the equally dramatic view of Central in the background.

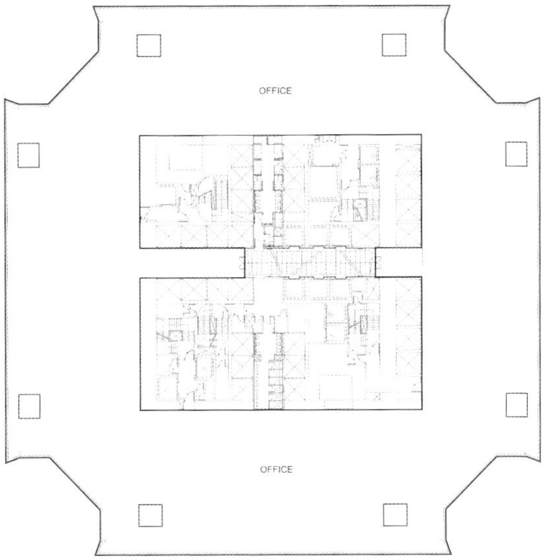
OFFICE
OFFICE

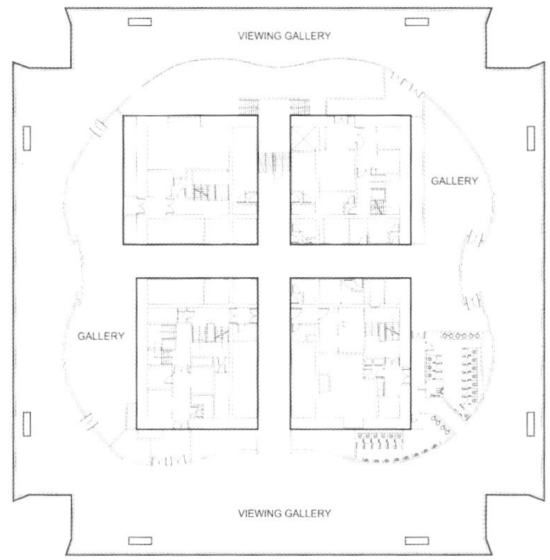
VIEWING GALLERY
GALLERY
GALLERY
VIEWING GALLERY

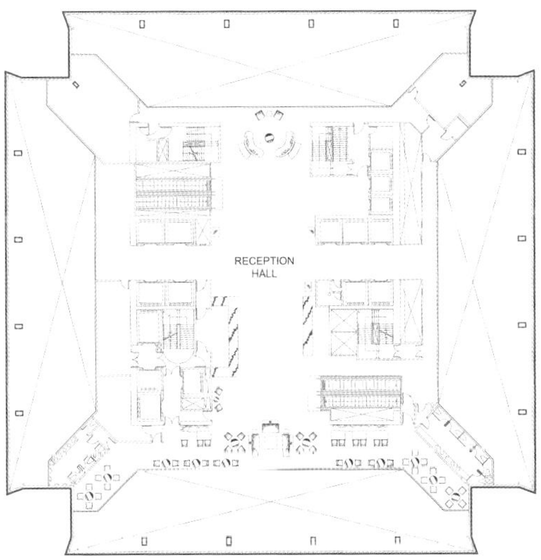
RECEPTION HALL

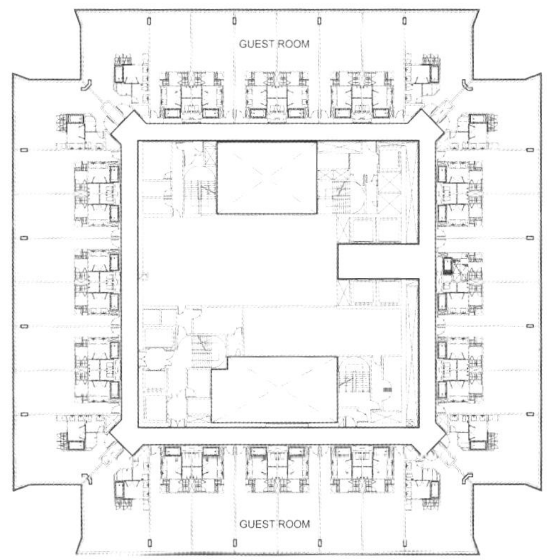
GUEST ROOM
GUEST ROOM

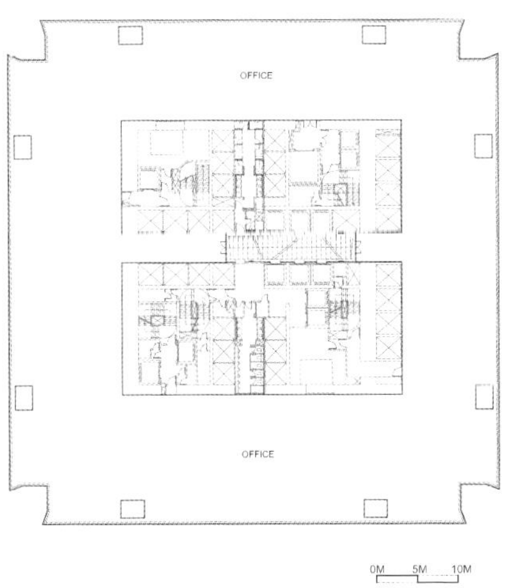
OFFICE
OFFICE
0M 5M 10M

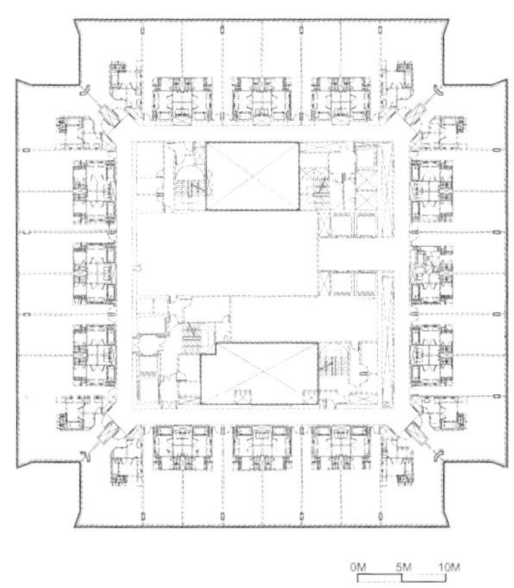
0M 5M 10M

6/

CONSTRUCTING BUSINESS SENSE

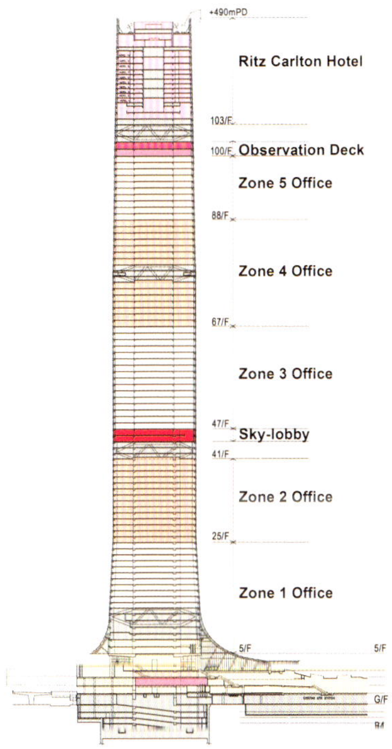

It may be argued that ICC is just as much an engineering feat as an architectural one. It is currently the ninth tallest building in the world and the tallest building in Hong Kong. sky100 indoor observation deck is the highest indoor observation deck in the city. ICC was constructed in phases; work continued on the upper floors as tenants moved into the lower floors, an astounding achievement considering the sheer scale of the project. With different and sometimes opposing requirements from its various tenants ranging from hospitality to retail to corporate, ensuring that each group's unique requirements were addressed proved to be challenging. Sun Hung Kai Properties considered ICC a vessel: sometimes it would contain water and sometimes it would contain wine. Engineering flexibility into the building to allow for different occupants was vital. Plus, as a super tall skyscraper, health and safety were of paramount concern in a region prone to destructive typhoons.

"There is more engineering involved in commercial buildings, especially super high rises," states Kenneth K.F. Mo. "For example, the lift system is very demanding. As a builder, we need to know about steel, curtain wall and building services. While commercial buildings employ steel construction, residential buildings are mostly concrete work and more about the interior finishing. ICC is game changing: it not often we get to work on a building of its height."

In a city that revels in its cloud piercing skyline, tall buildings may seem passé. Yet the taller the building, the greater the risks and the more care is required to ensure the nuts and bolts of the structure works. Hong Kong is one of the world leaders in super high structures and in maximising plot ratios. The city also knows a thing or two about mix-use developments and the utopian concept of living, working and playing in the same place, just as in the Chinese villages of the past.

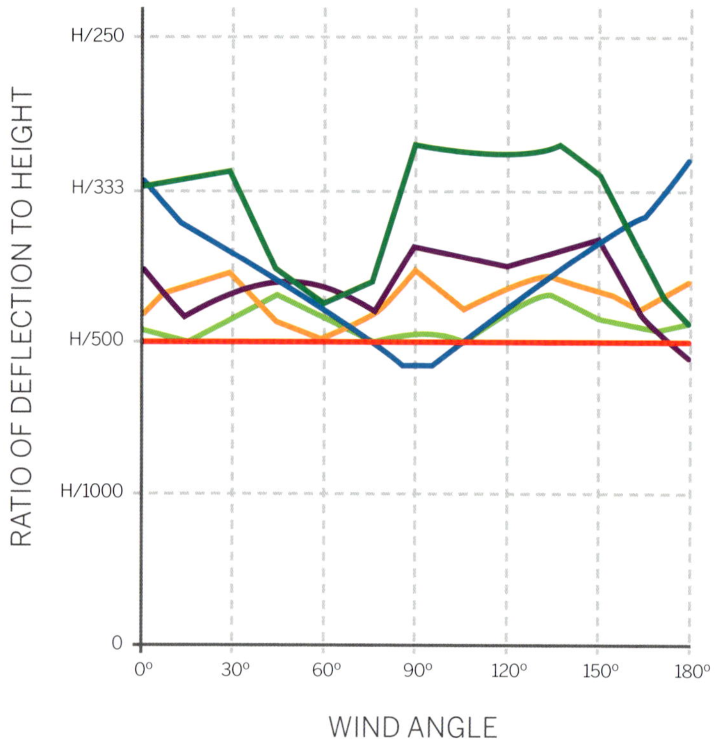
H/250
H/333
H/500
H/1000
0
RATIO OF DEFLECTION TO HEIGHT
0°
30°
60°
90°
120°
150°
180°
WIND ANGLE

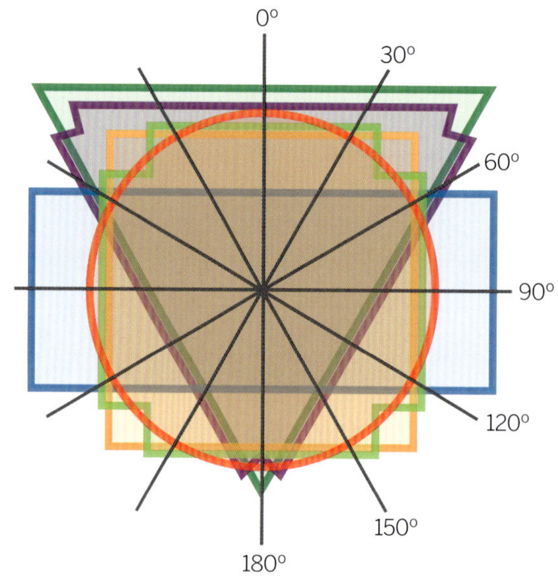
0°
30°
60°
90°
120°
150°
180°

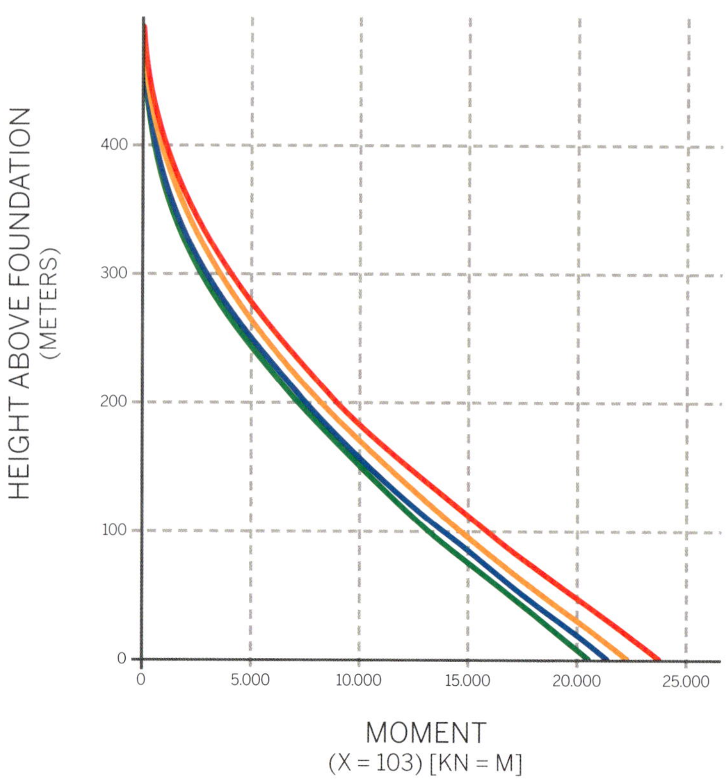
HEIGHT ABOVE FOUNDATION
(METERS)
400
300
200
100
0
0
5.000
10.000
15.000
20.000
25.000
MOMENT
(X = 103) [KN = M]

Opposite page: (clockwise from top) Various forms were considered before KPF and SHKP eventually settled on a square plan with notched corners as the best solution for ICC; a wind diagram shows that the most stable form for ICC was a square in plan with its corners cut out at 90-degrees; in elevation, a moment diagram shows that one of the most stable profiles for the building is an elegant barbell shape that nips in slightly at its centre; how wind would affect the different forms; and the ratio of wind deflection relative to the building's height.

Above: ICC's final form gently tapers at the top to provide a stable sense of well being for guests in The Ritz-Carlton, Hong Kong at the very top of the building.

"Structure is important but, in some ways, it is passively driven," says Philip Lai, director with Arup, the structural engineering consultant for ICC. "While architecture is attractive to people for its aesthetics and planning, and building services can provide occupants the facilities and comfort it requires to conduct their daily business, the structure of a building is often less appealing and, therefore, less appreciated by occupants and passersby. However, without the correct structure in place, the infrastructural frame of a building may not be safe or comfortable for its occupants. Though structural elements are often hidden behind finishes and façade, good structural design help the realisation of the architect's vision. It helps building services to function well without compromising safety of the building."

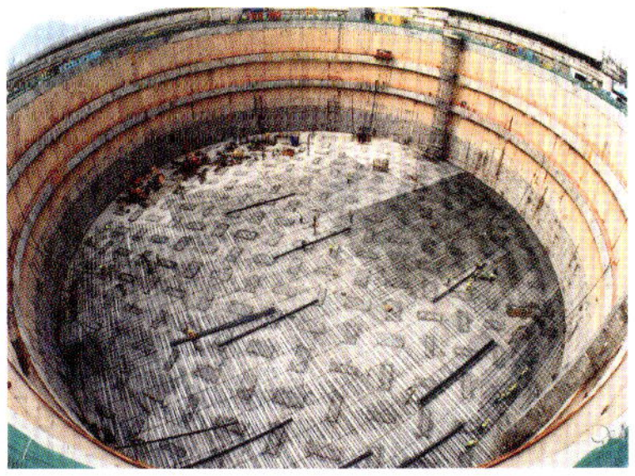

Opposite page: Completion of the circular diaphragm wall and excavation, showing the relative positions of the completed shaft grouted barrettes. The circular diaphragm under construction is ideal for resisting stress and allows the existing rail lines underneath to continue operations.

Far left: Rebar fixing for the pile cap construction.

Left: Rebar fixing for the core walls and basement elements.

Below: A view from within the diaphragm wall of rebar fixing for the pile cap construction.

ICC is located in a geographical region with deep bedrock profiles, buried between 60 and more than 130 metres below ground. Typically, Hong Kong's tall buildings have pile foundations brought down to the bedrock. However, ICC's site has a deep and varying bedrock profile, which poses great difficulty and risks to the piling work. The building required hundreds of piles to support its gravity loads and to resist the lateral wind loads. Even a theoretical five percent defect ratio for piles exceeding 100 metres in length would be unacceptable. "That's too big a risk," says Lai. "If the piles are 90 metres or deeper, one defective pile may delay work for six months until it is fixed. If there are several that need remedial work, the cost to such a large scale project is colossal. We wanted a better guarantee in terms of quality of piles."

After months of study, Arup decided to adopt what was known as a shaft grouted barrette, a type of friction pile that did not require it to reach bedrock. Instead of bearing on bedrock, it is supported by the friction between the pile and the surrounding soil. Using a diaphragm wall technique, bentonite slurry was used to fill the trench as excavation was proceeding to stabilise the cut face of the trench. "Upon reaching the toe level, a series of skillful tasks including placement of reinforcement cage, de-sanding and replenishment of fresh bentonite slurry followed prior to concreting," says Lai. "The bentonite slurry was then displaced as tremie concrete was being placed. The displaced bentonite slurry was pumped to a storage facility and reused later for ongoing excavation on other barrettes.

"Before tremie concrete was placed in the barrette, grout tubes, tube-a-machette, were installed within the reinforcement cage, with a total of eight per barrette. Six were to be used for grouting with the other two as spares in the event of blockage. Within 24 hours of concreting, water under pressure was pumped through each machette to burst the concrete. This would create a path for the future grouting work. After the concrete set, roughly between 10 to 14 days, grout was injected under pressure into the sides of the barrette to force the soil back for a layer of grout between soil and barrette. The technique enhanced the friction capacity between the soil and the barrette, and improved the load's carrying capacity, allowing it to be constructed only down to 70 metres

below ground and not deeper. It is a very secure foundation system for the building. And it is more economical too."

For the existing MTR to continue operating smoothly adjacent to the site as ICC's pile cap and basement levels were under construction, Arup used a circular diaphragm wall as the lateral support and barrier. "A circular form by nature is a good mechanism for resisting stress. It gave us the confidence that the MTR operation would not be jeopardised," notes Lai. "Whenever movements due to excavation exceeded a certain threshold level, an alarm would go off and all site work had to stop until it was cleared by MTRC or the Buildings Department. For ICC, there was no such disruption as the lateral movement was less than the threshold."

Another huge challenge for the building was its stability above grade: both actual and as perceived by its occupants. Lai explains that tall buildings are susceptible to wind-induced sway oscillation. However, the same movement experienced at different frequencies will give occupants completely different feelings. "It's a game of structural analysis. The stiffness and mass of a building affect its natural frequency. It is important for the structural engineer to design a building such that its natural frequency is not sensitive to the prevailing movements of the building under the effect of wind loads. When movement occurs, it will be within the human comfort zone."

At one point, dampers similar to the ones in Taipei 101 were considered for ICC to increase structural damping of the building, but the idea was eventually abandoned. "Taipei 101 was designed to withstand severe earthquakes and dampers seem to be an appropriate measure," Lai explains. "It may also be a good business decision to enhance the attractiveness of the sky lobby with dampers. For ICC, we would rather save the client millions of dollars by designing the building without the need of any dampers. In the end, the stiffness of the building is sufficient to keep dynamic motion of ICC within its occupants' comfort zone."

To provide the building the required stiffness for stability and comfort, different structural form options were considered before the final form was adopted. In Hong Kong, for a mid-rise building of 30 storeys, the lift core would be enough to give the building its structural stability. Taller buildings, however, need something more complex, such as numerous small columns along the perimeter to form an external tube for the building. In the case of a building with ICC's height, even more is required for stability as otherwise deflections may be too large and movements may not be kept down to an acceptable level. ICC required a solid core, and outriggers at several levels connect the core to the mega columns to keep the building structurally stable and well behaved. "This configuration also gives the building expansive views of the horizon without obstruction between the mega columns," says Lai.

The mega columns at the perimeter of the building act like poles that a skier uses to help balance. The outriggers act as arms while the core act as the body of the skier. While the mega columns are coupled with the central core wall through the outriggers to enhance the building stiffness, the belt trusses act as the linkage between the mega columns in the perimeter planes. They help the perimeter frames act more efficiently, thus also making significant contributions to the overall stiffness. During the construction stage, the belt trusses provided temporary supports for floor construction, offering opportunities to simplify falsework and the construction process.

Opposite page, top left: Outrigger steel members being hauled up to the appropriate level for installation.

Opposite page, top right: ICC's outrigger system as it is being set into place at the core wall of the building. Instead of a traditional truss system, ICC's outriggers only reach a short distance into the building's core walls.

Opposite page, bottom: Installation of a structural steel joint at a mega-column for an outrigger.

Top: Construction of the basement in progress.

Above: Erection of the first tower crane for construction of the superstructure upon completion of the pile cap.

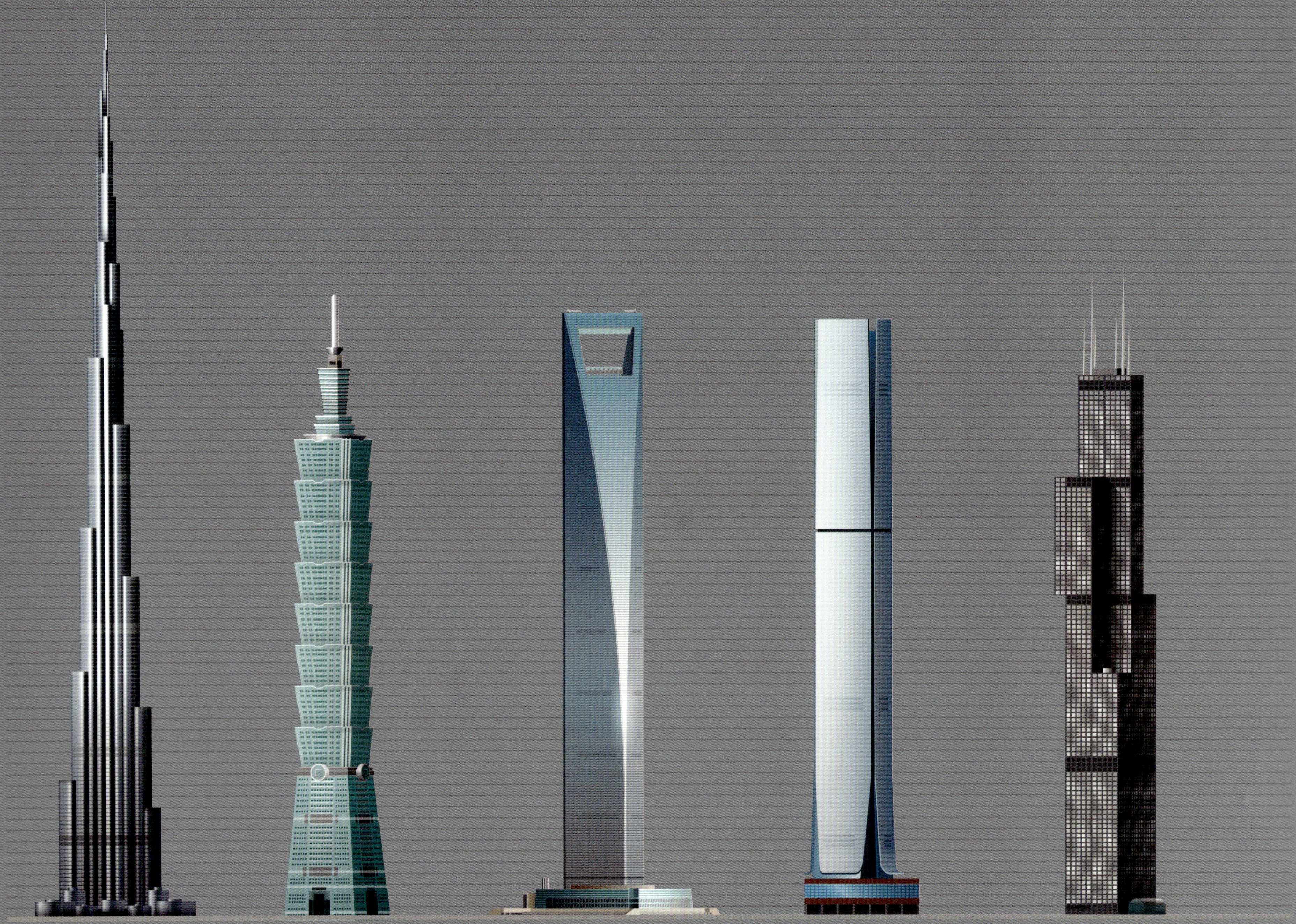

Burj Kalifa

HEIGHT
829.8 metres

LOCATION
Sheikh Zaied Road, Dubai

COMPLETED
2009

ARCHITECT
SOM

Taipei 101

HEIGHT
509 metres

LOCATION
Xinyi District, Taipei

COMPLETED
2004

ARCHITECT
C.Y. Lee & Partners

Shanghai World Financial Center

HEIGHT
492 metres

LOCATION
Century Avenue, Pudong, Shanghai

COMPLETED
2008

ARCHITECT
KPF

International Commerce Centre*

HEIGHT
484 metres

LOCATION
Austin Road, West Kowloon, Hong Kong

COMPLETED
2010

ARCHITECT
KPF

Willis Tower

HEIGHT
442 metres

LOCATION
Wacker Drive, Chicago

COMPLETED
1973

ARCHITECT
SOM

*Data on page was taken in 2013.

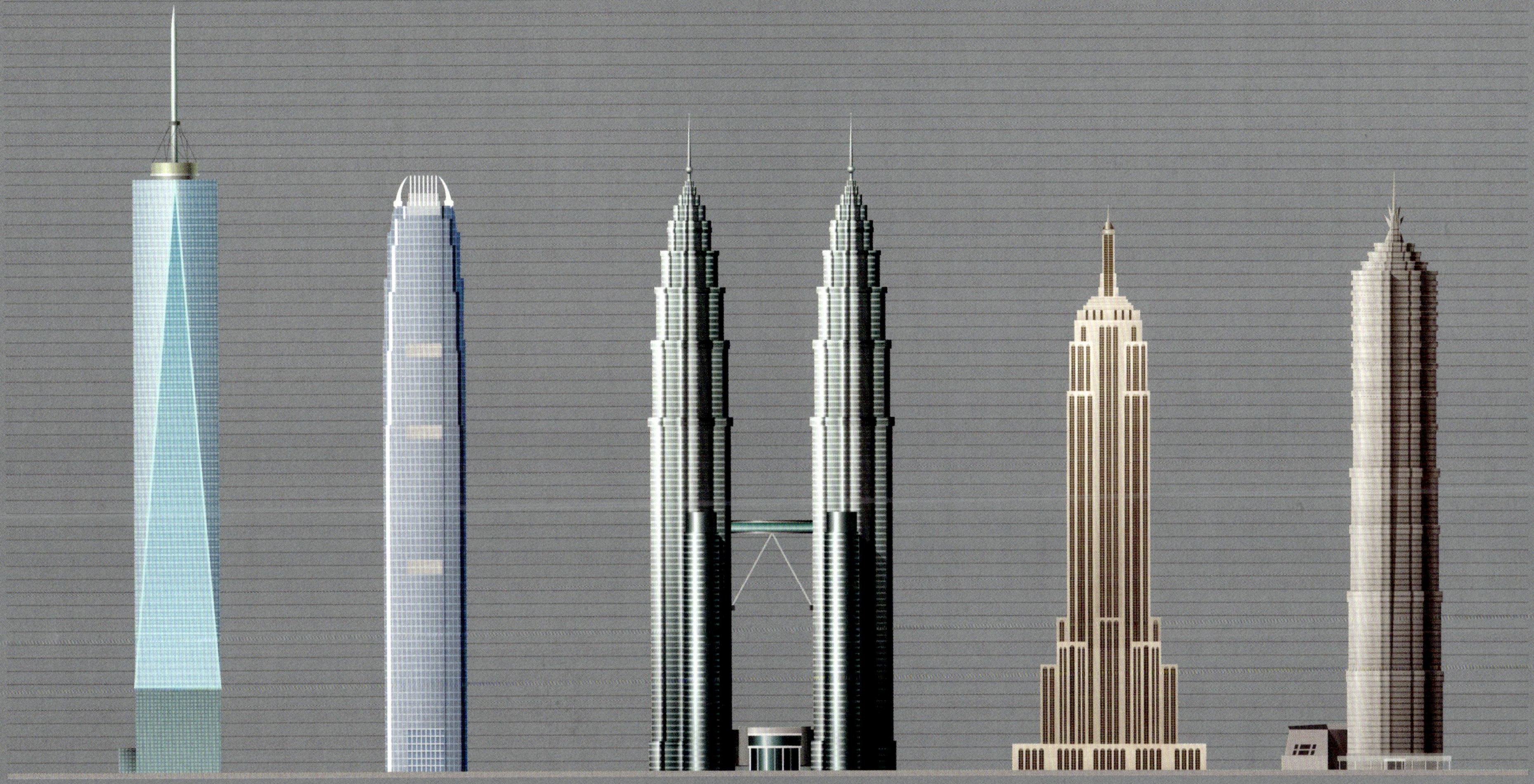

One World Trade Center

LOCATION
New York, NY

COMPLETED
2014

Two International Finance Centre

HEIGHT
415 metres

LOCATION
Finance Street, Central, Hong Kong

COMPLETED
2003

ARCHITECT
Cesar Pelli with Rocco Design Architects

Petronas Towers

HEIGHT
451.9 metres

LOCATION
Jalan Ampang, Kuala Lumpur

COMPLETED
1996

ARCHITECT
Cesar Pelli

Empire State Building

HEIGHT
443.2 metres

LOCATION
Fifth Avenue, Manhattan, New York

COMPLETED
1931

ARCHITECT
Shreve, Lamb and Harmon

Jin Mao Tower

HEIGHT
420.5 metres

LOCATION
Century Avenue, Pudong, Shanghai

COMPLETED
1999

ARCHITECT
SOM

Preceding pages: ICC stands as one of the top ten tallest towers in the world.

Right: A view from the West Kowloon Highway in the early evening with ICC and 2IFC against the background of Victoria Peak.

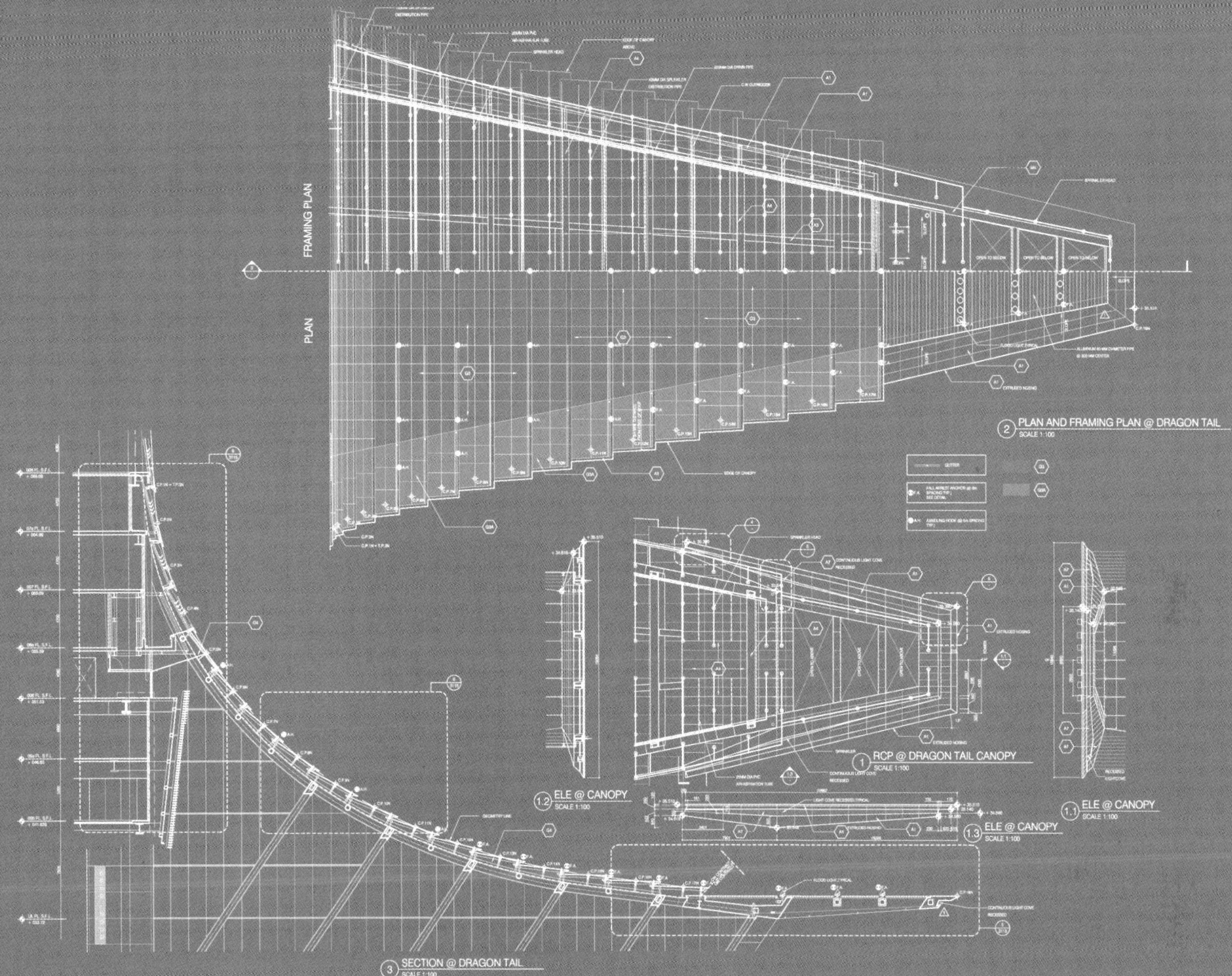

Opposite page: Various views of the dragon's tail while it is being constructed.

Above: Plans and elevations of the dragon's tail.

06 05 2009

Opposite page, top: A view from the roof of ICC of Central's skyline.

Opposite page, bottom left: Mega-columns along the perimeter of ICC support each floor that is being constructed.

Opposite page, bottom right: A lonely worker soldiers on at the very top of the tower.

Left: The bottom of ICC being clad with glass shingles as the core continues to rise during construction.

ICC's core is situated in the centre of the building and acts like a highway to allow for vertical transportation of goods and people. Structurally, the core is like the backbone providing the building safety and integrity. Generally, the best structural layout for a tall building is a core that is as square and concentric as possible, as in the case of ICC. Machine rooms, back of house facilities and secondary egresses such as staircases are all located inside the core, allowing for open and flexible space in the rest of the floor plate.

Arup conducted extensive research to find a concrete aggregate that provided the stiffness required for the mega columns and the building core. The study ended up with the selection of a volcanic tuff as one of the aggregates' components, producing a high strength and high modulus concrete that helped keep down the overall size of the mega-columns.

Arup also conducted studies and tests that helped reduce the conservative parameters in the previous wind code. "The government changed it based on our findings, and we could then proceed with our structural design using the reduced design wind speed," says Lai. "This resulted in less bulky member sizes, created more useable space and led to substantial savings in the cost of construction."

Instead of a traditional truss system as used for many other tall buildings which carries the steel truss members through the length of the supporting core wall, ICC's outriggers are designed to be embedded only for a limited distance into the core wall. "We didn't have to carry the structural steel truss through the entire length of the core wall," notes Lai. "The core wall contains a lot of rebars. With the truss spanning only between the core wall and the mega-columns, we've saved material and avoided rebar congestion. It would typically take three months to build one level of outriggers designed with traditional trusses; we shaved that to two months for ICC by using the simplified trusses. This is based on some of the lessons learned from Two IFC and we welcomed the opportunity to apply the improved version of trusses to ICC."

5
4
3

Opposite page: To accommodate the huge indoor cooling towers, the triple floor height for the mechanical plant room is over 15 meters.

Top: The Building Management System (BMS) Centre is set up for ICC to adopt control system architectures and philosophies to satisfy the need for advanced automation. It is the brain of building to integrate all building service elements to achieve energy savings and improve building operations.

Bottom: Ample essential generators installed in high level plant rooms are cornerstones of the highly resilient power supply system in ICC.

"ICC sets a benchmark in tall building design," says Lai. "What we have done is a useful reference for the structural design of tall commercial buildings. Others can use an outrigger system like the one we've designed. Although we had many sleepless nights and carried out extensive and thorough analyses, it was worth the effort we put in."

ICC's building services requirements needed to be engineered for a state of the art iconic building. "One of ICC's biggest challenges is to provide business continuity for its tenants," explains H.K. Yung, director of mechanical and electrical consultant, J. Roger Preston (JRP). "That was important for banks and financial tenants. We wanted to make the building highly efficient, business friendly, with a full fit out design that was flexible. For example, considerations for further expansion and re-stacking have been taken into account in the design. This allows flexibility for tenants to carry out fit-out works to suit their business needs at minimum cost and the least business interruption."

For the tallest skyscraper in Hong Kong, the building services system are precisely designed to offer premium quality services for the building and to serve the occupants in the most economical and energy-efficient manner. Reliability, resiliency and redundancy of the building services are of paramount importance to a world class skyscraper operating in good condition and high efficiency all year round.

Yung acknowledges that vertical transportation is a challenging topic for super high rise building. As more lifts are added, they take up a considerable amount of gross floor area—balancing the ideal number of lifts while maximising the floor plate's available leasing area and floor to ceiling headroom is always a compromise. Extensive coordination meetings with architects and structure engineers have been carried out in order to achieve the optimal floor to ceiling height, and to accommodate all mechanical and electrical equipment in the tight ceiling void.

For ICC, various strategies and approaches were adopted to achieve a flexible and expedient elevating service. To increase the efficiency of the

Top left: To harmonize the building envelope design, 11 units of tailor-made cross flow horizontal discharge type indoor cooling tower are installed in ICC to serve the office floor. The indoor cooling tower is currently the largest in Hong Kong.

Bottom left: Sophisticated lift destination control system which maximizes the efficiency of double-deck lifts and boosts their handling capacity by 15%.

Opposite top: Dedicated and 100% backup essential generators are provided for banks and financial tenants for supporting their mission critical equipment.

Opposite center: Computerised power monitoring system enables the estate management to monitor the whole power supply system in real time and operate the system in the most efficient manner.

Opposite bottom:
Left: Fire Services Pumping System provides sufficient hydraulic pressure for sprinkler system to serve the high-rise office floors.

Center: Heat Pump Plant enables the effective plume control of indoor cooling tower plant.

Right: Emergency air cooled chillers provide secondary chilled water supply source for essential air conditioning area, such as computer room and data centers.

building core, a sky lobby approach and double deck lifts were adopted for passenger lifts. To achieve the maximum efficiency from double-deck lifts, a destination control system was applied to enable the lift control system to analyse the demand holistically in real time, and assign the most appropriate lift deck to serve the passengers in the most efficient manner. This boosts the handling capacity by 15 percent, which enables a good balance between the waiting time in lobby and riding time in lift car. It ensures that an optimised elevating service is provided.

For the electrical system, siting the transformer substations (70MVA in total) on above ground mechanical floors where the major M&E plant are located, was the most effective way to contain voltage drop and distribute electricity to the plant and tenants. This arrangement also tied in with the plan of phased occupation to ensure the availability of power supply in a timely manner.

ICC boasts two high efficiency water cooled centrifugal chiller plants, comprising of six 11kV chillers in the lowest mechanical floor to serve the office zone and five chillers in the upper mechanical floor to serve the The Ritz Carlton, Hong Kong. As the office portion exceeds 400 metres in height, hydraulic zoning is one of the design's greatest challenges. Hydraulic break by plate type heat exchangers was carefully and strategically located to avoid excessive pressure on the air handlers and to ensure optimum chilled water temperature and chiller efficiency. Dual risers groups, each comprised of three chilled water pipes, were installed for the office floors to give the highest system reliability and resilience.

To harmonise the building envelope design, 11 units of tailor-made innovative crossflow horizontal discharge type indoor cooling tower were installed for heat rejection of the air conditioning to serve the office floor. It is currently the largest indoor cooling tower plant in Hong Kong. In ICC, the pre-treated fresh air rate was designed to satisfy the Excellent Class IAQ objective proposed by Hong Kong's Environmental Protection Department and ASHRAE 62.1 standard to provide a healthy indoor environment for the occupants of the building.

In addition, JRP considered and developed various intelligent control strategies and energy saving opportunities for energy optimisation during the design stage. The strategies implemented include optimal

KOHLER.
POWER SYSTEMS
KOHLER

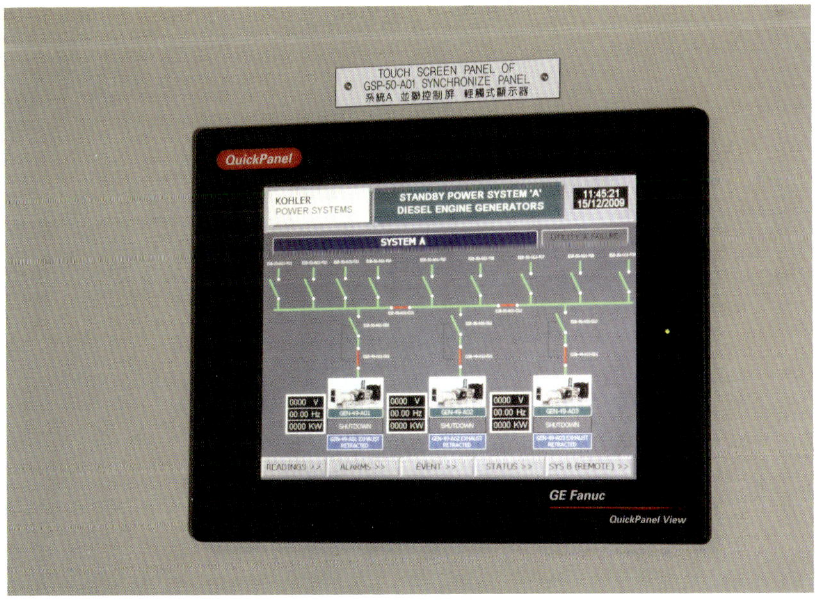
TOUCH SCREEN PANEL OF
GSP-50-A01 SYNCHRONIZE PANEL
系統A 並聯控制屏 輕觸式顯示器
QuickPanel
KOHLER
POWER SYSTEMS
STANDBY POWER SYSTEM 'A'
DIESEL ENGINE GENERATORS
11:45:21
15/12/2009
SYSTEM A
GE Fanuc
QuickPanel View

H.W.R.
CDWS
CDWS

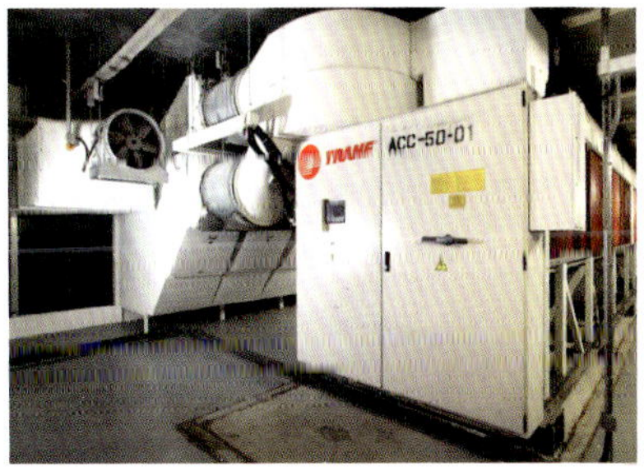
TRANE
ACC-60-01

Top left: Large Cooling Tower axial fans are installed at the high level of indoor mechanical plant room to avoid air short circuit.

Middle left: ICC boasts a high efficiency water cooled centrifugal chiller plant which comprising of six 11kV chillers in the lowest mechanical floor to serve the office zone.

Bottom left: The chiller tube cleaner machines are installed to remove the scale accumulated on the inner surface of chiller tube automatically in order to maintain high efficiency.

chiller and cooling tower sequencing control, water pressure differential set-point control, AHU supply air static pressure reset control and DCV-based fresh air control, and chilled/cooling water temperature set-point reset strategies. The initiatives resulted in reduced energy consumption, with an impressive amount of electricity saved.

"Leakage and solar transmission from the curtain wall could impact the air conditioning system seriously," says Yung. "That's why, in order to reach a balance of daylight access and energy efficiency, we spent a lot of effort liaising with the curtain wall consultant to establish the thermal insulation efficiency and air tightness requirement to lower the energy bill and capital investment, while maintaining a comfortable and high quality working environment for ICC's occupants."

The phased occupation of ICC proved to be a bold move for Sun Hung Kai Properties, as two thirds of the building was still being constructed when one third of it was occupied. "This affected every aspect of the project," says Tony W. M. Tang. "The vertical stacking of ICC meant that extra safety arrangements due to fire and other catastrophes had to be in place."

"During the phased occupation stage, we have to make sure that the temporary fireman's lifts were provided in each phase to cope with the fire services requirements for the occupied floors," says Yung. "Temporary fire service tanks and pumps had to be provided to support the fire service installations for the occupied floors prior to the completion of the permanent equipment in the higher levels. Transformer rooms were designed to tie in with the programme of phase completion to ensure power supply was available in a timely manner.

"We would like to emphasise that ICC is an engineering feat integrated with quality, sustainability and innovation. There was no way that we could take credit for such a successful project; it had to be team effort. Although there were many difficulties encountered during the design and construction process, it was a great experience for all of us to be part of Hong Kong's landmark project."

In Year 2012, JRP was awarded Quality Building Services Engineers of the Year for its work on ICC.

Right: An elevation of ICC shows what is housed on each level.

Following pages: The view looking down the southwest façade of ICC is spectacular and vertigo inducing all at once.

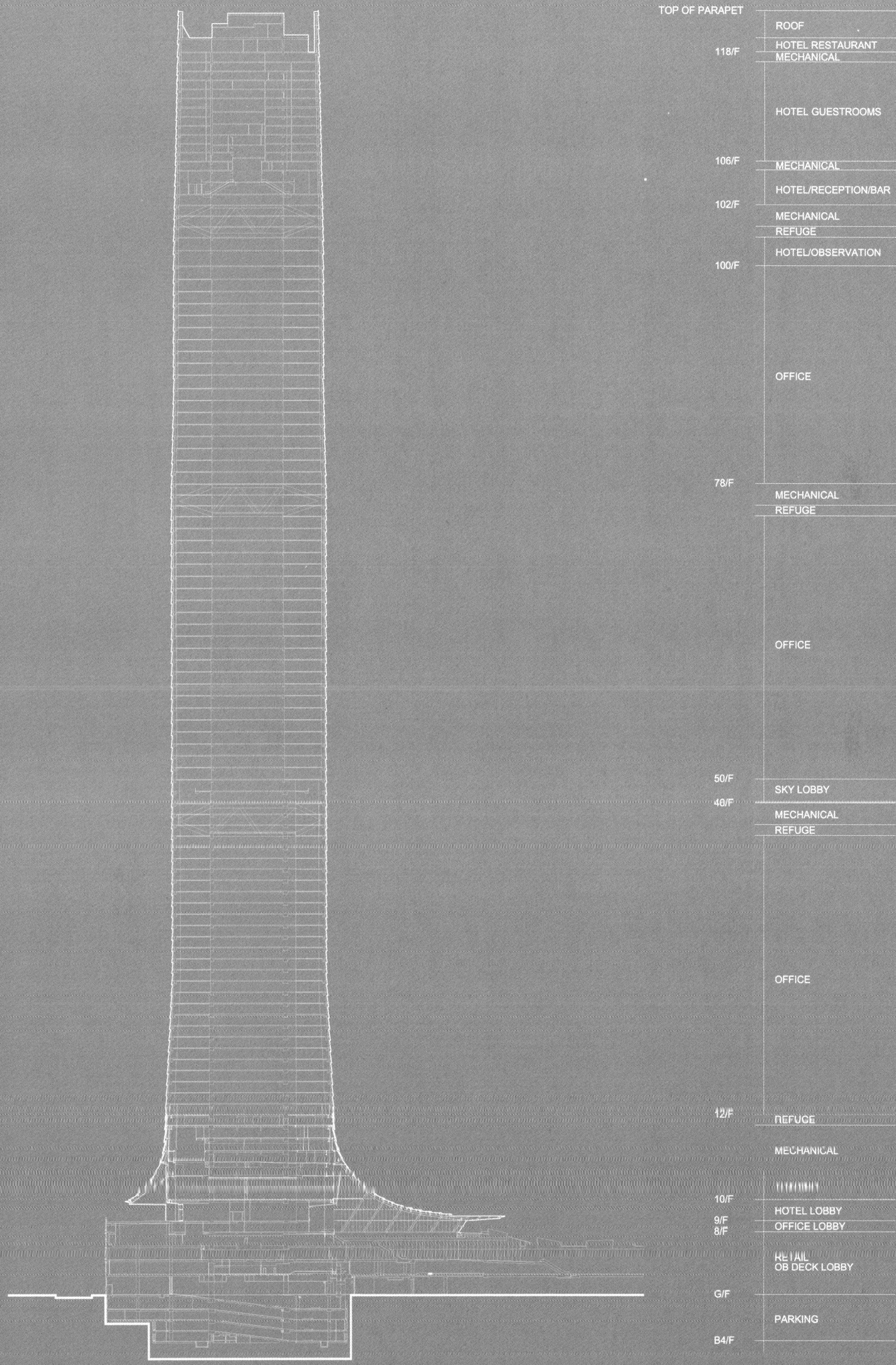

ICC: Moving on Up

How an iconic building is occupied in phases even while it is being built

Opposite page: Double Deck Lift with advance lift destination control system provides flexible and expedient lift services to all tenants. The streamlined profile of lift cars enables tenants to enjoy quiet and comfortable journeys inside high speed Double Deck Lifts.

Two noteworthy attributes of ICC became evident during the final construction period: its state-of-the-art vertical transportation system and its ability to allow for phased occupation.

All of the consultants understood the need for a holistic approach: combining new lift technologies with an intuitive strategy for circulation and way-finding. They worked closely with the lift contractor, Schindler, on 85 lifts that were designed to provide vertical transportation for more than 20,000 people, with capacities of up to 4,500Kg and speeds approaching nine metres per second.

ICC's double decker lifts are the first usage ever of this typology, and remain the largest application of double decker lifts in the world. The comprehensive system of high tech digital input displays and turnstile smart card readers linked to dispatch controls streamline traffic flow. An advance lift destination control system analyses passenger demand in real time to boost handling capacity by 15 percent compared with other systems. As there are separate passenger lifts and corresponding lift lobbies for office floors, observation deck and The Ritz-Carlton, Hong Kong hotel, passenger flow is better managed. Sky lobbies on the 48/F, 49/F and 88/F ensure efficient crowd handling and shorten the wait time, and their usage is closely monitored. For example, if there are more people arriving than leaving, departure trips will be prioritised, reducing the transport of passengers to sky lobbies to stem overcrowding.

For ICC's office tenants, proximity smartcard access control to office floors and secured areas maintain a high level of security control. Dedicated VIP lifts are served by a private and secure VIP lift lobby. For uninterrupted and discreet back-of-house services, dedicated service lifts are provided for office floors, observation deck and The Ritz-Carlton, Hong Kong to efficiently transport goods and waste. A 4,500Kg service lift allows for transportation of power companies' transformers as required, as well as heavy equipment or furnishings during tenant relocations. Strong winds encountered during typhoons will be picked up by building sway sensors; when necessary, the lifts susceptible to building sway will reduce speed or park at pre-determined floors if there is a posed danger to its passengers.

Sun Hung Kai Properties determined that early handover for newly signed tenants anxious to move in meant that the building had to be occupied in phases. While construction continued on the upper floor zones, the lower floor zones would be fully operational with tenants conducting their daily business. The phased occupation occurred in separate stages in 2008, 2009 and 2010, with two temporary occupation permits and one full occupation permit issued for ICC respectively each year. Contractors still working on the site had to provide adequate technical and safety training, allowing building management staff to operate the facilities properly. Naturally, the two parties had to work quickly to complete defect rectification work within a reasonable period.

To facilitate the phased occupation, a 400 metre tall temporary external access tower was erected on the northwest corner of the ICC site to provide an efficient means of transporting workers and materials to upper level construction sites while the lower floors were being occupied by tenants. After each temporary occupation permit, ICC's block of lower levels had to be released to tenants while the tower climbed upwards.

All suspended working platforms—commonly known as gondolas—were designed to be installed on the main roof at a height of 480 metres. To facilitate cleaning and maintenance for the occupied lower floors during the phased occupation, two gondolas were placed temporarily on 80/F at a height of 320 metres.

The continued construction on ICC meant that safety and noise control became more critical after the first temporary occupation permit. During construction work on occupied floors, fireproof walls and acoustic enclosures were implemented to separate the two areas and prevent dust, fumes or noise from disturbing the tenants working on those floors. Temporary fire service lifts were provided after each phase's completion to meet fire services requirements for the occupied floors, along with temporary fire service tanks and pumps prior to installation of permanent ones on the higher levels.

Quiet construction methods included expensive concrete saw-cutting rather than noisier hydraulic breaking for concrete modification work. Some of the work was carried out after regular business hours or during holidays to minimise disturbance. A temporary acoustic enclosure was erected around the two high-capacity concrete pumps on 9/F. In addition, all water and concrete pumping pipes passing through occupied floors sat on vibration isolators to mitigate noise and vibration transmission. Above ground power substations on mechanical floors allowed for energy efficient distribution of power during the phased occupation. Advanced liaison with power companies, the Water Supply Department and telecommunications operators allowed for smooth supply of these services to tenants as soon as they moved in.

ICC's phased occupancy would not have been possible without careful planning, cooperation and advanced technology implemented by its talented team of engineers and engineering consultants.

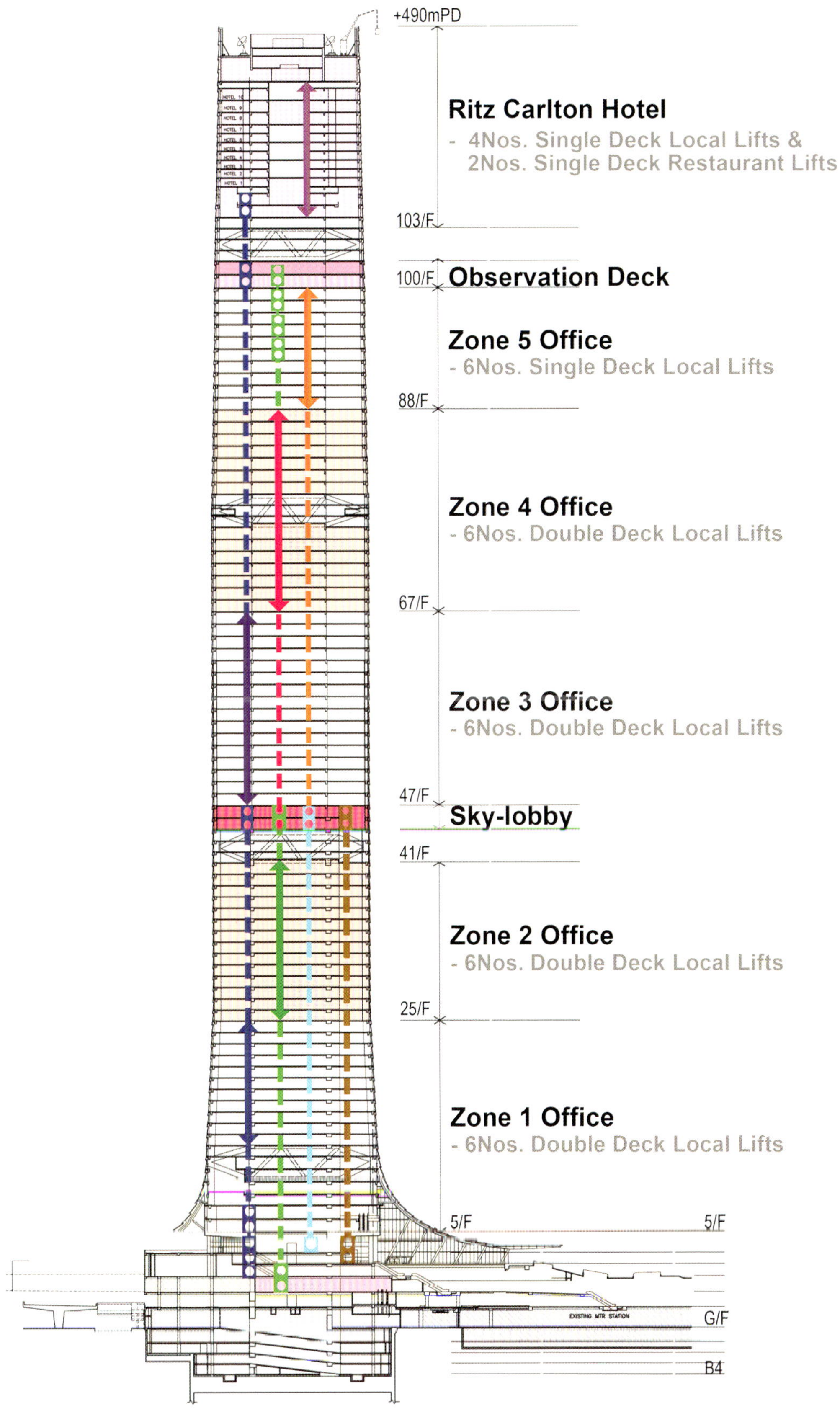
+490mPD
Ritz Carlton Hotel
- 4Nos. Single Deck Local Lifts &
2Nos. Single Deck Restaurant Lifts
103/F
100/F
Observation Deck
Zone 5 Office
- 6Nos. Single Deck Local Lifts
88/F
Zone 4 Office
- 6Nos. Double Deck Local Lifts
67/F
Zone 3 Office
- 6Nos. Double Deck Local Lifts
47/F
Sky-lobby
41/F
Zone 2 Office
- 6Nos. Double Deck Local Lifts
25/F
Zone 1 Office
- 6Nos. Double Deck Local Lifts
5/F
5/F
G/F
B4

77

HOUSING FINANCIAL HEROES

If ICC was indeed a vessel that may contain anything from water to wine, its current directory reads like fine champagne. It was not a matter of if you build it they will come, either. When Sun Hung Kai Properties first began developing ICC, it had modest ambitions. It knew that it was building a tall building—the tallest in Hong Kong when completed and one of the top 10 in the world. But the developer was honest: Central was where financial tenants wanted to be. A Central address had the cache of being a part of the iconic skyline that gives Hong Kong its dynamic buzz. Efforts to diversify businesses away from Central even to other parts of the island only work for certain types of businesses. International financial services companies would never dream of moving away from the established network of grade A offices, restaurants and clubs where they have always conducted business. With a little luck on its side, ICC proved that kind of thinking to be debatable.

"It was a matter of timing," agrees Tony W.M. Tang. "The market was with us when we first began approaching potential tenants. Many firms suffered from inefficient operations because they were spread out all over Central. They had a long list of grievances about their current landlords and facilities. They had to go somewhere. But Central no longer had real estate for companies to expand their premises.

"Morgan Stanley wanted to move into IFC at first. Even if we shifted existing tenants around, we were only able to clear about 120,000 square feet for them. We never thought that they would all move to ICC. But the company saw that it was a modern building that allowed room for their staff to grow there. The facilities could be tailor made since the building was still under construction. The timing was perfect. If ICC was constructed two years earlier or later, Morgan Stanley wouldn't have moved across the harbour. But its lease was expiring and it needed the space. The lower floors of ICC were able to accommodate their move even though the upper floors weren't ready yet. Their traders were able to continue trading safely."

Top left: The porte cochere for ICC's tenants is a sophisticated welcome for guests and staff arriving for appointments.

Bottom left: Vehicular approach to ICC includes a panoramic view of the premises as drivers head up to the podium level from the city's key arteries.

Opposite page: Lit signage direct visitors to the various drop off points at ICC, facilitating clear and informed wayfinding regardless of the time of day.

To foster the deal, Sun Hung Kai Properties was committed to helping Morgan Stanley with fitting out the space to their specific technical requirements. Part of that encompassed a new transformer room designed and constructed for the bank. It converted office space into mechanical areas and upgraded the building's infrastructure. "Although ICC is a grade A office building, some tenants feel that it is still not enough," says Tang. "They want a Formula One car, not a Ferrari. Banks like Morgan Stanley do 24 hour business and cannot be interrupted. For example, data and voice had to continue even if the power grid is down. We ensured that it can continue for hours, just like an airport or hospital or train station." 12 months after signing the agreement, Morgan Stanley moved in—a quick turn around even for a completed building.

Another method of enticing anchor tenants is to give them distinct and separate identities, including their own entries and concierge desks. As Morgan Stanley was the first major bank to move out of Central, it expected a great deal in return for taking the leap. When it first visited ICC's site, some of its executives had never ventured beyond Tsim Sha Tsui. They arrived in limousines. "Morgan Stanley was quite clear in terms of what they wanted," recalls K.W. Lo. "They had their own interior designer. Morgan Stanley sees itself as a trailblazer."

The Asian chairman for Credit Suisse met with Lo, who explained his vision of the kind of connectivity ICC can provide. The two came to a mutual understanding. The banker aimed for a phase three move into ICC to allow more time to plan out their facilities. "They just wanted everyone together," says Lo.

Deutsche Bank
Morgan Stanley

Above: ICC's three anchor bank tenants each has its own reception desk and concierge to welcome VIPs.

Meanwhile, Deutsche Bank was beginning to outgrow its former premises as well and its requirements were exceeding what its landlord could provide. It intended to construct facilities adequate for 10 years of growth and allowed the appropriate budget to do so to exacting standards. "Technically, Deutsche Bank knew what it wanted," notes Lo. "It asked for different ways to expand for future arrangements."

Lo admits that he could have targeted more conventional companies such as traders that have simpler technical requirements and not so many sacrifices needed to be made. Yet he stuck to his guns because he knew that he had a product financial services firms valued. With ICC still under construction and with the knowledge gained from leasing Two IFC, Lo was able to tailor many aspects of the building to his anchor tenants' wish list criteria.

Today, several years after the topping out of ICC in 2010, the building has built up momentum. Lo and his team of leasing agents do not have to sell West Kowloon anymore: the district is beginning to sell itself. Morgan Stanley occupies 16 floors while Credit Suisse and Deutsche

Bank take up 12 floors each; the latter has the option to expand to a full 18 floors written into its lease. Newer tenants such as Standard & Poor's see the benefits of being part of a connected network weaving transportation and business that ICC provides. It is a significant shift away from business as usual in Central that has never previously taken place in the history of Hong Kong, nor in such a short time span.

"ICC has become like a vertical Wall Street," says Tang. "Currently, 15% of Hong Kong trades happen in the building. It has become a hub that is changing the neighbourhood. Many residents in West Kowloon are staff who work in ICC and lease or buy in the area. We always envisioned the district to be a good place for business, but we never imagined it would reach this kind of status so quickly."

Above left: Following the dragon's tail, ICC's tenants head out for a bite on a sunny business day.

Above right, top: A stunning double height panel of art graces the internal staircase of Deutsche Bank's offices at ICC

Above right, bottom: Staff and guests utilise the main set of escalators that connect Elements shopping mall with the tower; they are operational 24/7, as the escalators also allow access to The Ritz-Carlton, Hong Kong.

Above: Stately signage displaying the anchor tenants' logos greets guests and staff along the drive to ICC's porte cochere.

Right: ICC's lift lobby is split along two levels to quickly and efficiently shuttle tenants to their respective floors within designated lifts.

LOBBY
H
70 72 76 78 80 82 86

Opposite page, right: Anchor tenant Morgan Stanley's reception area at ICC.

Opposite page, bottom left and right: Deutsche Bank's lobby features bold sculpture that complements the space's design.

Right: Morgan Stanley's staff canteen at ICC.

Bottom left: Another view of Morgan Stanley's staff canteen at ICC.

Bottom right: Colourful graphics add life to a series of meeting room walls at Deutsche Bank.

Above: A view up the inside of the dragon's tail showing the entrance to ICC's various office tenants' lobbies.

Right: Day or night, the access to ICC from Elements shopping mall teems with staff, shoppers and visitors to the city.

London: City of London to Canary Wharf

With Ken Shuttleworth, founder, Make Architects; former partner, Foster and Partners

London's east end has long had the stigma of being the wrong side of town. Its docks along the Thames, once thriving for most of the 19th century, saw decline by the mid-20th century and were closed by 1980. Canary Wharf, situated in the West India Docks on the Isle of Dogs, was deemed to be an ideal location for a new central business district to take the burden off the City of London.

Masterplanned by American architect Skidmore, Owings & Merrill (SOM) and developed by Toronto-based Olympia & York, the first building completed was One Canada Square. At the time it was unveiled in 1991, it was the tallest building in the United Kingdom. Then the bottom fell out of the London property market and Canary Wharf stagnated. Slowly, by the mid 1990s, it recovered and interest in the area grew. The opening of the Jubilee line in time for the city's millennium celebrations helped connect the district with the rest of the city. Today, it is generally regarded as a success story for how to create a new financial hub.

London-based Ken Shuttleworth witnessed the changes in Canary Wharf's development while he was working as a partner with Foster and Partners in Hong Kong on projects including the HSBC headquarters and the Hong Kong International Airport at Chek Lap Kok. In 2004, he founded Make Architects and continues to work on design-driven buildings in the United Kingdom and Asia.

"Canary Wharf is massively successful," he says. "There is a nice tension between the City of London and Canary Wharf. It started off as commercially led, part of the 80s big bang when companies wanted big floor plates and American style buildings. These big American law firms couldn't find the space they needed in the City of London. Canary Wharf acted as a pressure relief valve. Now, it is much more mixed. There is a huge amount of shopping and a lot of people live there. It's like a modern city with an American flavour."

Shuttleworth recalls the days when the future for Canary Wharf wasn't so rosy. "When it opened, its biggest problem was no tube line reached it," he remembers. "People could hardly walk there. There were no roads, no transportation. The government promised a new tube line called the Jubilee, but it was delayed. There was a lull between when the buildings were completed and when they were actually occupied. The development also had financial problems due to the economic downturn. Citibank gave it a reboot with a 20 storey tower that gave confidence to the rest of the market. And when the Jubilee line finally opened, it became very successful."

Shuttleworth sees the two financial centres of London as being complimentary, as they offer different things. "Canary Wharf is simple, efficient, economical and straight forward. Many buildings were designed by American architects and landscape architects, such as Cesar Pelli and I.M. Pei. There were little or no planning constraints which provided developers and designers alike with a blank canvas and more freedom. Meanwhile, the City of London's rich historic context with strict planning restrictions and many constraints made it more challenging for developers and designers to find the right solution that would fit and compete within its complex surroundings. As a result, the City of London's skyline has become a bit of a shape race."

Over time, Canary Wharf's personality has emerged and can be attributed in part to the extracurricular life that it enjoys. "There are now cinemas and theatres, which are a

good start to building Canary Wharf's cultural programme. Make is working on some small scale kiosks that will add life to the streets. The shopping there is of good quality with some top end brands, and it works as a pedestrian friendly destination. The Canary Wharf development is the first of its kind in England, and it has been successful."

Despite Canary Wharf's evolution into a lively hub, Shuttleworth believes that many businesses still prefer to be in the City of London. "There is a greater buzz in Central London. There is free wifi everywhere and a lot of business is being done outside the office. People enjoy meeting in coffee shops, especially for confidential meetings. The nature of work has changed and people can work anywhere. But they still like going to an office where they can meet people and flirt. It's a more enjoyable social event." While technology or design based firms stick to the west end of the city, financial institutions like the wide spaces of Canary Wharf. "Many banks have their own buildings there," notes Shuttleworth.

West Kowloon faces similar changes to Canary Wharf 30 years ago, as it is an incomplete puzzle that is currently heavily skewed towards finance. "The challenge for West Kowloon is to make it not just about the amount of office space it offers," says Shuttleworth. "When West Kowloon Cultural District opens, there will be a lot more cultural activities for people who want to spend time there. It's also about the infrastructure. Transportation is a big key to the area's success. The express rail link is already in a good place. It is also a challenge to blend ICC with its surroundings more. Many mainland Chinese want to be in Hong Kong and they have a huge amount of investment dollars that they can spend with the city on their doorstep. No doubt China's influence upon the world is immense. Hong Kong's development market can enhance this business coming from mainland China."

8/

FOSTERING MALL CULTURE

On a typical Tuesday evening in the southeastern end of Elements, children are zipping around an ice rink playing in a friendly hockey game while their parents cheer on. Above them on terraces that overlook the rink, movie goers are lining up for a preview screening of the latest blockbuster at The Grand Cinema. In Three Sixty supermarket, shoppers are picking up jet fresh produce for a gourmet meal along with fresh baked goods to accompany. Dotted among the luxury brand boutiques from Europe and North America, there are electronics shops and specialty stores that cater to home accessories. And whether it is fine dining or a simple burger and chips, there are restaurants, cafes and take away shops for any and all appetites.

West Kowloon was not always so bustling. A dozen years ago, the retail area adjacent to Kowloon Station was much smaller and was for several years occupied by Dickson Warehouse Outlet Centre. With the entire area a massive construction site and difficult to access by foot, traffic was low. The area's lack of natural lighting further took away from an enjoyable retail therapy experience.

But that changed when Elements was unveiled above Kowloon Station in 2007. Designed by Benoy, it offers one million square feet of retail space. One side offers direct access to Kowloon Airport Express station and the other to Kowloon MTR station. There is a through bus terminal offering routes directly into numerous mainland Chinese cities within Guangdong province.

Elements gets its name from the five elements found in nature. Each of Elements' five zones is themed after an element and contains related design details. For example, the wood zone contains sculpture that resembles tree branches and the water zone contains a nine metre high vertical water feature. It offers more than 120 shops including the largest cinema in the city, The Grand, with a total capacity of 1,600 seats. Elements' popular ice rink is available for ice hockey games and figure skating lessons—and is a magnet for parents and children wishing to cool off on a hot summer day.

The roughly doughnut shaped shopping mall offers a number of distinctive services for Hong Kong retail outlets. Its public washrooms, for example, all include a waiting area in between the male and female

Top left: Shoppers are spoilt for choice at Elements, the shopping mall underneath ICC, as it contains all the international and homegrown brands they desire.

Top right: With its variety of restaurants, bars and cafes ranging from luxury to takeaway alongside its retail diversions, Elements is a go-to spot for a girls' afternoon out.

Opposite page: The entry to Kowloon MTR and Airport Express stations at the base of ICC makes it convenient for residents to get around the city—and beyond.

sections with seating and stocked magazine racks. There are dedicated nursery rooms for moms to nurse babies in privacy. Valet parking is available in addition to self service parking.

When it first opened, Elements was focused on high end outlets and brands with an emphasis on fashion. It had a quiet beginning, with shoppers still needing to be convinced to leave Central or Tsim Sha Tsui. Its circular layout was confusing to some. Yet over time and after ICC's tenants began moving in, the mix changed and now includes a more diverse range of products, services and dining. It was important for not just the senior executives to have places to shop and dine, but also for entry level staff and middle managers to enjoy an affordable lunch or run errands on their breaks.

"The dragon's tail points to the centre of the mall," says Tony Tang. "The plaza created there is well integrated with the design of the mall. There is good synergy between ICC's tenants and the mall's facilities. Elements has seen a gradual evolution. We were informed by one of our tenants that his staff needed a mix of dining, cafes and fast food, and stationery shops, pharmacies, gyms and retail banks. It didn't need more high end shops. In the beginning, the mall set the bar too high with luxury brands. Staff working in ICC had to take taxis to Yau Ma Tei to have lunch." Today, there is more selection for take away products such as bakeries and fast food for staff to eat at their desk or on a quick break. Even supermarket Three Sixty offers an increasingly wider variety of salads, sandwiches and rice boxes for those living and working close by.

Civic Square, the podium level piazza with mid-end and fine dining restaurants, is a prime example of how Elements has been shaped by

Above left: Even from within ICC, the branded offerings at Elements entice with their distinctive logos and arresting window displays.

Above right: Spacious aisles and a mixture of brands make shopping at Elements a family affair.

Opposite page: Two arcs comprise Civic Square's food and beverage offerings, and what better way to enjoy them than on a sunny day on its patio?

ICC's population. When it opened in 2007, it contained mostly high end restaurants that struggled to find their niche clientele. The outdoor space in the centre of the restaurants was perfect for al fresco dining, yet it was empty most of the time. The quiet vibe did little to entice diners seeking lively destinations to spend a few hours, despite the prestigious names adorning signboards with their promise of excellent cuisine. After ICC's tenants began moving in, Civic Square's restaurant and bar mix began to see more affordable options with patio seating. Asian and international cuisines are available there and the atmosphere is more dynamic.

As shops and tenants evolve, so will Elements' relationship with ICC. One thing is certain though: the two will continue to support each other while ensuring that West Kowloon becomes a neighbourhood district in its own right.

malouf's
DIAMOND

West Kowloon: Life and Lifestyle

With Kevin Chan, Homeowner and Resident, Sorrento, West Kowloon

Investment banker Kevin Chan explains why he chose to purchase a property in West Kowloon and what he loves about living in the neighbourhood.

Ever since Kevin Chan returned to Hong Kong in the 1990s after emigrating to and living in Toronto for more than a decade, he has resided in Kowloon. He spent his early childhood years with his family in a Mei Foo Sun Chuen flat and though he has worked in Central's big banks, he has always preferred Kowloon's attractions.

"A lot of people who live on the Hong Kong side think it's more sophisticated to have a Hong Kong address," Chan says over coffee at Elements' L'Atelier de Joel Robuchon. "And there are plenty of Kowloon residents who aspire to live on the Hong Kong side. I never had this desire."

Currently, Chan manages the investment portfolio for a family-owned private equity firm whose office is based in Cheung Sha Wan—his first job in Kowloon. Due to the nature of his work and the frequent client visits that he must conduct, lifestyle was the driving factor for selecting a home as opposed to close proximity to his office. "I have always liked this area," he says, referring to the Tai Kok Tsui area and the more recent reclaimed land developments. "For me, location and price were the biggest factors when we were looking to purchase a property. At the end of 2008 due to the Asian financial crisis, we saw the best prices ever for some of the city's best properties. I bought our 1,400 square foot Sorrento apartment when the market was at rock bottom in 2009."

Sorrento is a luxury residential development situated on the northern end of the Union Square site. Completed in 2003 and designed by Wong Ouyang, it encompasses five 60 to 75 storey towers with a footbridge that provides direct access to Elements shopping mall, Kowloon Station and the Kowloon stop for the Airport Express. Chan's three bedroom unit offers broad views to the west. On a clear day, sunsets are particularly dramatic over Victoria Harbour looking out to Lantau Island. "The view is important to me," he says. "When I saw the apartment for the first time, the sun was setting. It was impressive. Even now, when I come home from work in the evenings, I still am awestruck by how beautiful Hong Kong can be."

Chan lives in the apartment with his wife Rebecca and her parents. The family completed a mostly cosmetic renovation of the property upon possession, converting one of the bedrooms into a study. "My in-laws are very active, independent seniors," he says. "My wife has two older sisters and my mother-in-law often visits her grandchildren during the day. My father-in-law will go to a club in Kowloon Tong to play mahjong with his friends. They often go on mini-holidays to various towns and cities in Guangdong province, and they love the convenience of being able to take the cross-border buses downstairs at Elements directly to their destination. We usually have dinner together. My mother-in-law enjoys buying groceries from the Yau Ma Tei wet market—she doesn't mind making a special trip there. And we like going to the old shops under Mei Foo Sun Chuen to get fresh seafood from fishmongers that we have known for years."

Chan finds living in Sorrento very convenient, not only in terms of transportation and proximity to Union Square, but also due to the many services that it offers. "Our concierge desk will take care of our dry cleaning. The podium that connects all five towers is very comfortable. If we are too lazy to

drive over to Midlevels for our regular walks up to The Peak, we will stroll downstairs along the podium to get some exercise after dinner or on weekends. Our clubhouse offers activities such as yoga and there's a decent swimming pool."

Chan also takes advantage of all the services and facilities within Union Square. "We used to shop more at IFC Mall, but since we moved here, we go there much less and prefer to stay at near home and shop at Elements. After all, a store is a store. We tend to watch films at The Grand, the cinema in Elements. The facilities are very good, and much better than many other theatres in the city. If we are dining out, my favourite restaurant is Tosca in The Ritz-Carlton, Hong Kong. We go there for dinner and brunch. We have tried a few of the restaurants at Sky Dining 101, too, such as the Japanese ones. And we have attended events held so far at West Kowloon Cultural Centre, such as the Wine & Dine Festival."

Being a banker himself, Chan understands their preference for being in a prestigious location. "It's a mental hurdle for offices to move to Kowloon," he acknowledges. "I think that in terms of moving to ICC, sectors such as the bean counting accountants and brand conscious lawyers won't do it. And right now, it's just ICC—that's a limitation. We need more of an office mix. Once XRL opens, there should be more office buildings for a true financial hub. I believe that West Kowloon should be considered an extension of Central. ICC is a class A office building and it's only one MTR station away from Central."

HOUSTON
11

El Pomposo

Ristor nte Italiano

9/

PUTTING ON THE RITZ

The Ritz-Carlton, Hong Kong was already an established brand in the city well before the doors opened on the 102th floor of ICC in March 2011. The U.S.-based operator previously managed a purpose built hotel in Central from 1993 to 2008. With the hotel occupying prime real estate in Central, it eventually followed the direction of its neighbours Hilton and Furama, and was demolished to make way for a grade A commercial office tower. The Ritz-Carlton building's disappearance from Central paved the way for its beloved restaurants and legendary services to find a new envelope in a purpose built property that was equally as good as its previous home. The brand's cachet meant that not just any place would do; it had to be a home that would be able to match the luxurious niche that the operator enjoys as an international 5-star hotel. The Ritz-Carlton, Hong Kong did just that by securing the top chunk of ICC.

Tim M.T. Mak, architect and assistant project director with Sun Hung Kai Properties Real Estate Agency, believes that it was a gutsy yet natural move across the pond. "People enjoy the experience of going to The Ritz-Carlton," he states. "They enjoy the service there. In Central, the hotel had a different clientele. It was a small property and close to Mandarin Oriental. Barristers and solicitors used the function rooms for specific size events and had a little world of their own there. But at ICC, the ballrooms and function rooms can host many different activities. It's a different clientele, too. We see more Chinese visitors than the old Ritz. Chinese visitors seem to enjoy the views and West Kowloon—they will come for the sake of that."

The Ritz-Carlton, Hong Kong sits on the top of ICC and occupies levels 102 to 118. When it was completed, The Ritz-Carlton was the world's highest hotel with the world's highest indoor swimming pool on the 118th storey. Although that record has since been broken by J.W. Marriott Marquis in Dubai and will most likely continue to be broken as buildings top out increasingly higher, the hotel nevertheless commands an awe-inspiring panorama. With 312 rooms nearly half a kilometer above ground, the hotel challenged structural engineers Arup to come up with a stable design that could withstand the city's strong wind conditions. During the humid summer months when typhoons wreak havoc, signals eight and above means that business shut down and staff goes home. Public transportation grinds to a standstill and ferries are cancelled. Yet hotels must stay open. "The tolerance of acceleration is lower for a hotel since people stay in their rooms during typhoons," notes Mak. "The core's design would be different if ICC was purely an office building."

The ballroom and function rooms were also considered at one point to be grouped with the other food and beverage outlets at the top of the hotel. Instead, they were separated and positioned at the base to better facilitate traffic flow and due to their lack of need for natural light. "This allowed for panoramic views for the restaurants on the 102th floor," says Mak. "We also had in mind some kind of public facility initially at the top, such as an observation deck. It was our wish to have some kind of access to the outdoors from a high level. O-Deck was a planning gain for this building." Ozone, the bar on the 118th floor, offers an outdoor terrace that looks eastwards towards Central, Causeway Bay, east Kowloon and beyond. The curve of Victoria Harbour around Hong Kong island is easily discernable from this vantage point and is a unique perspective to ICC.

"Many people have some kind of preconceived idea of what the Ritz-Carlton brand represents," says Mak. "People associate it with a New England style. When we approached the hotel's design, we discovered that a lot of those preconceptions weren't true. In fact, Ritz-Carlton has a lot of stand alone modern buildings. The brand respects local cultures. As ICC's architecture is modern, there was no fixed style and nothing to impose. The architecture affected the interiors."

Singapore-based LTW Designworks was responsible for most of the hotel, while Tokyo-based Wonderwall designed Ozone. "Masamichi Katayama of Wonderwall had never done this type of bar before," says Mak. "He is known for his retail work. But by looking at his portfolio, we could see that he designs unique things for shops that would suit us."

Originally, the restaurant floor was going to contain two outlets and meeting rooms, but the final design boasts three: Italian restaurant Tosca, Michelin-starred Cantonese restaurant Tin Lung Heen and all day dining The Lounge & Bar. "We found that there were never enough private dining rooms available in restaurants," says Mak. "This way, the three restaurants can share them. Meeting rooms are interchangeable; we could open them up and make them more flexible, thereby maximising the usage for each outlet and making them more efficient."

The hotel's presidential suite, known as The Ritz-Carlton Suite, contains a blend of grand and cozy spaces to make guests feel at home despite its 4,460 square foot, two bedroom spaciousness. Along with its large living and dining room, there is also a private spa with Jacuzzi in the generous stone-clad bathroom. "We want the stay for our guests to be a very personalised experience," says Vivian Li, The Ritz-Carlton, Hong Kong's former director of public relations. "The Ritz-Carlton Suite guests enjoy a personal butler, 24-hour limo service and monogrammed linens and bathrobes. The bathroom has a private sauna within it. The suite is like a mini version of the hotel."

"ICC is the kind of building that inspires aspiration," believes Mak. "The architecture speaks for itself. There's no need to sell it. The building's quality was what enticed the operator to make the leap to West Kowloon."

Opposite page: The Ritz-Carlton, Hong Kong welcomes guests with conical sculpture in the centre of its porte cochere.

Top right: The indoor infinity edge swimming pool on the 118th floor of The Ritz-Carlton, Hong Kong has the distinction of being one of the highest swimming pools in the world.

Bottom right: The Lounge & Bar is one of three fine dining options available on the 102nd floor of The Ritz-Carlton, Hong Kong.

Top left: The highest bar in the world when it opened, Ozone's singular look and feel is courtesy of Tokyo firm Wonderwall Design.

Top right: A wall of water and central glass sculpture offer a visual feast for diners enjoying a meal at Tosca, the Italian restaurant on the 102nd floor of The Ritz-Carlton, Hong Kong.

Above: With its striking light effects and deep lounge seating both indoors and on its terrace, Ozone is a popular spot for the city's well heeled.

Right: The Premier Executive Suite in The Ritz-Carlton, Hong Kong offer splendid panoramic views of Central and 115 square metres of luxury.

Opposite page, top left: The Carlton Suite in The Ritz-Carlton, Hong Kong is a 180 square metres corner room with a separate dining and living area.

Opposite page, top right: The living area within the Premier Executive Suite, The Ritz-Carlton, Hong Kong.

Following pages: The Ritz-Carlton, Hong Kong greets guests arriving by car with stunning views of the city's skyline as soon as they disembark.

EPSON

SHUN TAK
ageas

5-Star Dining

With Paul Lau, Chef de Cuisine, Tin Lung Heen, The Ritz-Carlton, Hong Kong

Guangzhou native Paul Lau is the commander-in-chief of one Michelin star Tin Lung Heen, one of the world's highest Cantonese fine dining establishments.

In 1977, 14-year-old Paul arrived in Hong Kong and got his first job within one week. Working as a busboy in Lung Yu Seafood Restaurant, he spent his last half hour every night teaching himself how to cook, after all the others had gone home using kitchen scraps so that no one would notice any missing ingredients. During his infrequent holidays, he would go to fellow chefs' home to learn how to make dim sum or siu mei—the succulent roast meats that he later became famous for.

"By the time I reached my early 20s, I had already learned a lot," Paul recalls. At the age of 22, he was hired to be the head chef at Lychee Garden, a Chinese restaurant in Johannesburg. He followed that with a stint in Dubai's International Hotel. Then, as China began to welcome chefs to helm its burgeoning 5-star hospitality establishments, he worked in both urban hotels and far flung resorts in Guangzhou, Wuhan, Beijing and Shanghai, including Beijing's Peninsula Palace Hotel.

"I never thought I would be a chef," he admits. "At first, I thought of it as a job, albeit a good learning experience. I always thought that cooking was a great profession. It's like being the conductor of an orchestra. Then, as I gained experience, I became more sensitive to flavors. And in different parts of the world, where tastes and cultures differ, I had to stand behind my dishes and present them as the definitive way a classic should taste."

One of Paul's best selling dishes at Tin Lung Heen is char siu, the savory sweet roast pork dish found in every barbecue shop across the city. "I use Iberico pork, with no added colour or soda," he reveals. "The pork is inherently very juicy—no need for tenderisers. Since the pigs feed on fruit, the pork bears the fragrance of fruit." Other signature dishes at Tin Lung Heen include double boiled chicken soup with Brazilian fish maw in a baby coconut and steamed crab claw using giant Vietnam crab with egg white and hua diao wine. "I created all these dishes specifically for Tin Lung Heen," says Paul.

His kitchen at Tin Lung Heen was specially designed for the 102nd floor space at ICC, with two areas concealed behind decorative screens so that guests can see activity but not the sometimes chaotic energy in a bustling Cantonese kitchen. "By dividing up the kitchen into different areas, we produce healthier and more hygienic dishes," he believes. "They are easier to manage. And since we are situated so high up in the sky, there is less likelihood of fire spreading quickly if all the fuel is separated."

Paul believes that his team of 24 staff member's best asset is their ability to work together. "The most important component behind a successful restaurant is the people working there," he states. "We all must be willing to communicate and cooperate."

My 48 Hours

8:00 AM	Get up, eat two cordycep mushrooms while reading dailies: *Apple Daily* and *Hong Kong Economic Times*. Iron clothes for the day
10:00 AM	Arrive at Tin Lung Heen
11:00 AM	Morning briefing with staff followed by lunch in Tin Lung Heen staff canteen
12:00 PM	Prepare for lunch hour rush
3:00 PM	Go to pied-a-terre on Battery Street in Jordan for some rest; stop off to say hello to teenage son working at Papi's in Civic Square
5:00 PM	Back to Tin Lung Heen for dinner hour rush
6:00 PM	Dinner in Tin Lung Heen staff canteen
10:00 PM	Go home
9:00 AM	Take mother, wife, and teenage son and daughter to dim sum breakfast at Loong Yuen in Holiday Inn Golden Mile
11:00 AM	Stroll along Canton Road
1:00 PM	Shop at Elements: 7 for All Mankind for jeans, Ermenegildo Zegna for silk scarves, The Regent Shop for custom made trousers and shirts
3:00 PM	Browse Yue Hwa Chinese Products Emporium in Jordan to add to large antique Chinese artifact collection
5:00 PM	Look at traditional Chinese walk-up tenement flats for investment in Jordan and Mongkok
8:00 PM	Dinner at home with family

10

SOMETHING FOR EVERYONE

One of the lessons Sun Hung Kai Properties learned after developing Two IFC was that the public loves tall buildings. Many commercial super skyscrapers such as Chicago's Willis Tower (formerly known as Sears Tower) and Taipei 101 offer an observation deck close to their summit that gradually became one of their host city's must-see tourist attractions. While Two IFC is strictly reserved for corporate tenants, ICC is more open and welcoming to the general public. It achieves that image with two floors that act as its public face: sky100 Hong Kong Observation Deck (sky100) and Sky Dining 101, on the 100th and 101st storeys respectively.

sky100, the city's only indoor observation deck offering 360-degree panoramic views, was designed by Benoy with visitors to Hong Kong in mind, though locals may discover something they didn't know about their hometown. It gives them an overview of the city through an immersive experience that is part exhibition and part sightseeing tour.

Sun Hung Kai Properties was careful to ensure sky100 had its own dedicated facilities spread over different levels near the base of ICC. On the ground level, tour buses allow groups to access sky100 directly upon arrival. Tickets are available through a dedicated box office on the first floor, while the main entrance to sky100 is a floor above. Thoughtful details such as a variety of coin-operated lockers for visitors' usage make sky100 a worthy stop in a packed day tour.

The journey to sky100 includes a number of installations such as a glass floor showcasing a three dimensional model of Victoria Harbour and ICC's relationship to its neighbours. A fleet of Hong Kong's fastest double decker lifts whisk visitors from the second to the 100th floor in 60 seconds. Lighting is kept intentionally dim and moody, for a stronger wow factor when the natural lights and 360 panoramic views welcome visitors as they step out into sky100.

In addition to the breathtaking bird's eye view of Hong Kong's matchless skyline from every angle, sky100 offers a number of different zones to engage the public. The 3D Hong Kong Story Theatre presents Hong Kong's rich history and the city's transformation from a humble fishing village into an international metropolis through a multi-sensory experience. Dotted across the floor are telescopes that can recreate day and night views along with special effects such as fireworks to help guests experience a well-rounded overview of the city. Rounding out the facilities is a customer service desk, a gift shop with branded sky100 merchandise ranging from plush toys to t-shirts, a photo booth to commemorate the visit with special background effects and a café. sky100 is also available for corporate and private events, including press events, corporate dinners, product launches, cocktails and weddings.

One floor above sky100 is Sky Dining 101. With its four prestigious restaurants catering to ICC's executives, local gourmands as well as international tourists, Sky Dining 101 has become a destination dining hotspot. Each restaurant also contains its own private dining rooms designed for private parties or business gatherings. The relatively shallow core to perimeter ratio allows for virtually every table to enjoy magnificent views of the city, with some tables near the core elevated to maximise sight lines.

Sky Dining 101 includes Japanese kaiseki restaurant Tengu Ryugin, Japanese robatayaki restaurant Inakaya, Cantonese seafood restaurant Dragon Seal and Shanghaiese restaurant Sky Crystal. All of these restaurants are unique and exclusive, tempting diners with scrumptious menus. In addition, each restaurant's operator had a proven track record in Hong Kong and provides alternatives to the dining options in The Ritz-Carlton, Hong Kong above.

Preceding pages, top: A view across Victoria Harbour in the early evening from ICC's sky100.

Preceding pages, bottom: The same view across the harbour on a sunny day offers a different kind of drama to locals and visitors to sky100.

Top left: Children learn how to use a telescope to see more clearly at sky100.

Bottom left: Visitors walk across a scale model of Victoria Harbour and iconic buildings on both shorelines as they arrive at sky100.

Opposite page, top: sky100 offers many educational displays that show the city's architectural development.

Opposite page, bottom: The vehicular drop off entry to sky100 leads directly to a ticket counter.

天際 sky100

DRAGON SEAL
INAKAYA

Opposite page, top: A private corner table at Japanese kaseiki restaurant Tengu Ryugin offers romantic views of the setting sun.

Opposite page, bottom left: The 101st floor life lobby of Sky Dining 101 with a view towards Inakaya restaurant at one end of the corridor.

Opposite page, bottom right: Art greets visitors upon entry to high end Shanghainese restaurant Sky Crystal.

Top: Visitors get a full sense of the city's extent as they look east from sky100.

Above: One of the notched corners allows uninterrupted views looking west towards Hong Kong's outlying islands.

Tengu Ryugin, a three Michelin starred restaurant in Tokyo, is the brand's first overseas branch. It strives to recreate the same type of ambience with natural textured stone and wooden screens. Founding chef Seiji Yamamoto works closely with chef de cuisine Hideaki Sato and his staff of five Japanese chefs to create a 10 course kaiseki set dinner based on seasonal ingredients flown in from Japan daily. The chef always surprises food lovers with twists on traditional Japanese cooking methods. Dishes presented are like works of art. With its exceptional quality and jet fresh ingredients, Tengu Ryugin has already been honoured with two Michelin stars after opening for merely a year.

Inakaya is designed to resemble an autumnal harvest and is decorated with sake barrels, dark timber furnishings and wenge flooring. With its signature grilled fresh products such as wagyu beef and Hokkaido kinki fish, head chef Masakazu Ushio draws upon the brand's 40 years of history in Tokyo with a full menu offering teppanyaki, sushi, sashimi, washoku and kaiseki. Beautiful details such as floral Japanese washi paper folded in the shape of a fan acting as chopstick holders enhance the dining experience.

Dragon Seal was founded by the highly decorated chef Wong Wing Chee, considered one of China's top 10 chefs. Its seasonal menu is inventive and plays upon traditional Cantonese dishes by giving them novel twists, such as stewed tofu and shrimp with black truffle and baked egg with purple yam caramel. The restaurant's design is contemporary and quirky, with wine glass chandeliers above the bar and a view down to sky100 some of its highlights.

Sky Crystal is a high end Shanghainese restaurant managed by the popular Crystal Jade group. Diners can savour authentic flavours derived from Huaiyang and Shanghainese cuisines through the restaurant's contemporary menu. Its light and airy interiors include crystal waterfall chandeliers and an abstracted Art Deco vibe. Its extensive wine selection includes French vintages that its sommelier can match with traditional Shanghai dishes such as hairy crab.

Fiona Chung, General Manager—Leasing Department at Sun Hung Kai Properties Real Estate Agency, remarks: "With the combination of breathtaking views of Hong Kong's cityscape, superb cuisine and stylish décor, Sky Dining 101 offers a truly memorable dining experience that cannot be found anywhere else in the city."

sky100 and Sky Dining 101 allow the city to experience ICC up close and personally, reaching out to a wide audience like a postcard that showcases its best qualities.

Opposite page: Japanese robatayaki restaurant Inakaya's open dining area affords direct views of Central.

Top: Inakaya's VIP room allows for 180 degree views of Victoria Harbour.

Above left: Seasonal ingredients are artfully presented at Inakaya's chef's table.

Above right: Barrels of aged sake greet guests at Inakaya's entry.

West Kowloon Cultural District: A celebration of the arts

When it is finally completed, the 40-hectare West Kowloon Cultural District promises 23 hectares of open green space alongside world class cultural venues designed by some of the most world's talented architects.

Hong Kong is often labelled as an efficient place for transportation and conducting business, but it rarely gets the thumbs up for culture. It is a somewhat unfair label, to be sure. Historically, long before the British came along, Hong Kong's New Territories and Kowloon were dotted with adventurous families whose ancestors had made their way south to establish a new way of life. These included a 12th century Song Dynasty princess, who sought refuge under an assumed identity when her father's throne was threatened. She lived hidden among the Tangs, the oldest and largest clan in Hong Kong, where she was eventually betrothed to one of its male heirs; they went on to spawn a new dynasty in Hong Kong, about as far from Beijing as anyone could be while still remaining in China.

The clans that arrived in what the English once called a barren rock brought along their ancestral traditions, including rituals practiced during important clan celebrations that take place today. Costumed parades and bamboo structures housing Cantonese opera, basin feasts and ancestor worship can still be enjoyed regularly. And it is no wonder that one of the highlights of the 40-hectare complex known as West Kowloon Cultural District (WKCD) is its bamboo theatre and tea house, designed by Canadian architectural firm Bing Thom Architects collaborating with Hong Kong-based architect Ronald Lu & Partners. Dubbed the Xiqu Centre to encompass all genres of Chinese opera, construction began in 2013 and it is slated to be the first major venue to open at WKCD, with 2016 its targeted completion year.

To generate buzz, former CEO Michael Lynch and his WKCD Authority (WKCDA) has previously erected pop up bamboo theatre structures upon its designated WKCD site for a period of four weeks to showcase Chinese and Cantonese opera. In early 2014, the structure's third edition was designed by Hong Kong architect Raymond Fung, and it was comprised of more than 12,000 bamboo rods. During the four weeks over the Lunar New Year that it was up and running, the temporary bamboo structure welcomed more than 100,000 visitors who enjoyed the various genres of xiqu—Chinese opera—performed live by the Chinese Theatre Associations' Plum Blossom Award Art Troupe. In addition, there were screenings of archival films showing past performances of the art form.

Also in the limelight are the continuing efforts by the team behind M+, the museum for visual culture. Swiss architectural firm Herzog & de Meuron won the design of M+ via competition; it is collaborating with TFP Farrells and Ove Arup & Partners Hong Kong on a target completion date of 2017. Similar to the Xiqu Centre, M+'s executive director Dr. Lars Nittve has led five Mobile M+ exhibitions across Hong Kong, with Building M+: The Museum and Architecture Collection one of its most ambitious shows to date. Held at ArtisTree between 10 January and 9 February 2014, Building M+ was a multi-faceted show that presented the competition entries submitted for M+ as well as M+'s collection of rare and archival material to date. Alongside a sketch by American architect Frank Lloyd Wright depicting a stairwell detail in Japan's Imperial Hotel dating back to around 1920, there were more current works by the likes of architectural photographer Iwan Baan's 2007 work showing construction labourers watching TV in the shadows of Beijing's Bird's Nest. The master plan for Mei Foo Sun Chuen—the largest housing estate in the world when first open—by Wong Tung & Partners circa 1973 illustrates what was to the first in a series of private housing estates, while

Hong Kong architect Tao Ho's model for West Kowloon hints at what might have been. Until M+ is open, Nittve and his team of chief curator Doryun Chong and architecture curator Aric Chen will continue to stir public interest with mobile exhibitions around town.

In May 2014, WCKDA announced that it had selected the architects to design the 1,200 seat Lyric Theatre, scheduled for completion by 2019. Dutch firm UNStudio won the commission in collaboration with Hong Kong's AD+RG. The Lyric Theatre will be the city's first facility dedicated to dance performances ranging from ballet to classical Chinese, as well as for opera, music and drama. Both Lyric Theatre and M+ will be situated on the western end of the district, with views facing Victoria Harbour. Freespace, an outdoor performing arts venue, created noise with the third edition of Freespace Fest, a pop up music and performing arts festival held in mid November 2014. These types of pop up festivals get the public involved while showing them the various types of performances and activities it can expect to enjoy at WKCD. Other venues slated for the district include a centre for contemporary performance, a medium size theatre, a music centre, a music theatre, a large size performance venue, an exhibition centre, creative learning facilities and art pavilions.

As the massive construction project will take up to another decade to complete, numerous organisations aside from WKCDA have taken advantage of the large plot of reclaimed land to host memorable events. From December 2009 to February 2010, WKCD was the site of the second edition of Hong Kong & Shenzhen Bi-City Biennale of Urbanism and Architecture. Hong Kong Tourism Board's Wine and Dine Festival took place at WKCD from 2009 to 2012, and Clockenflap Music and Arts Festival successfully completed its seventh edition in late November 2014. The latter featured more than 100 local and international bands, and is touted as Hong Kong's only outdoor music festival promoting indie and alternative Chinese music.

With WKCD in a state of flux for the immediate future, the activities and events taking place on the doorstep of ICC can only enhance the area's overall attraction as a self-contained and self-sustaining neighbourhood for living, working and playing. The synergy created by the two is a win-win scenario for all involved.

11/

OILING THE MACHINE

Super skyscrapers are akin to complicated machines, with interwoven systems that depend on each other and attentive, round the clock maintenance. ICC's management services team is responsible for ensuring that its diverse tenants are all satisfied and comfortable. At the same time, the team strives to enhance the building's facilities with a preventative approach to curb any potential problems. It runs ICC like a well-oiled machine and often the most important mechanisms are the ones least likely to be visible.

While ICC's commercial tenants may be aware that there are many lifts at their disposal, few may believe that the building actually contains 86 in total. It is the biggest vertical transportation system for a single building in the city, with more than 10,000 trips made daily. There are 24 double decker lifts to reduce waiting time, and it is the first double decker lift system in Hong Kong integrated with a personal card-based turnstile system to enhance security and exclusivity.

The lifts are monitored through a centralised 24-hour help desk in a control room that contains over 1,000 closed circuit TV cameras. There is a registered in-house nurse on standby, trained first aid staff equipped with automatic external defibrillators (AED) and first aid kits, ensuring that ICC is prepared for any medical emergency that may arise.

Many of ICC's tenants have met Brandy and Xanga, two English springers who have become lovable mascots for the building. They usually stand on lobby duty to welcome visitors and office workers in the morning as they arrive, at lunch and when they are leaving the office. The brother and sister team were born in England and are six years old; they have been at ICC since the building opened. Their main duty is to check the daily mail, sniffing out any irregularities. Their handlers Surya Gurung and Laxman Pun also take them on two hour training courses and walks throughout the Union Square podium; at night, the pair retires to a home in ICC's basement where they get treated to sausages and other doggie delights.

Top: A view towards Elements shopping mall from an upper lift lobby.

Above: Brandy and Xanga, two English springers, stand guard at Elements' entry to ICC with their handlers, Surya Gurung and Laxman Pun.

Opposite page, top: The shingles at the end of the dragon's tail becomes a stylised pergola.

Opposite page, bottom: The control room is dominated by a 24-hour help desk and more than 1,000 closed circuit TVs to monitor the 86 lifts servicing ICC's 110 storeys.

To keep ICC's glazing in tip top shape, five gondolas installed on the roof allow a façade inspection team and cleaners to access the top half of the building. There is also a material hoist that lifts curtain wall panes if they need replacement. Five more gondolas and two elevating platforms are tailor made for mid and low level maintenance, and are installed on the mechanical level above the 77th storey and at the eighth level's podium floor. For the dragon's tail, a soft rope system helps to minimise the gondola's swing caused by winds. Copper core wire ropes for power allows operators to control all functions while on board a gondola and from the main panel on the roof car above. To prepare for the unexpected, ICC's team equipped the gondolas with emergency kits and conducted emergency handling drills with the High Angle Rescue Team from Hong Kong's Fire Services Department to ensure that safety is always a priority. In 2012, the team was honoured with the Best Fall Prevention and Protection Programme by the Hong Kong Occupational Health and Safety Council.

ICC operates four dedicated shuttle bus routes for its corporate tenants to and from Kowloon Tong, Central, Tsim Sha Tsui and Kwun Tong during the weekdays. Tenants arriving via shuttle bus or taxi enter a dedicated lobby designed with leather seating and granite flooring scaled to feel comfortable both when empty and packed with people.

In keeping with Sun Hung Kai Properties' aspiration to go green, a number of initiatives have been implemented at ICC to involve tenants in sustainability awareness. Low carbon lifestyles through reduced energy consumption are encouraged through various energy savings and greening programmes.

The ICC Celsius 26 is one such example. This programme encourages tenants in ICC to set their indoor temperature 26 degrees Celsius or higher to reduce electrical consumption. In addition, the common areas of ICC are set between 24 to 26 degrees Celsius on specified days of the month.

Opposite page, top: Dedicated shuttle buses transport tenants' employees to key points across the city, including Central and Tsim Sha Tsui.

Opposite page, bottom right: There are designated parking spaces for ICC tenants that require car park.

Top: Commuters can await their shuttle bus from within ICC's generous lobby adjacent the shuttle pick up point.

Above: A main concierge helps direct visitors who are seeking information about ICC—or those who have lost their way.

ICC collaborated with The Hong Kong Polytechnic University to optimise its chiller plant operations. In 2011, the ICC team was the first in Hong Kong to achieve ISO50001 Energy Management System Certification, accredited by the Hong Kong Quality Assurance Agency. With these initiatives, the energy conserved measured up to a million kilowatts per year.

ICC's team encourages tenants to make use of the compost accumulated from a food waste decomposer installed in the building. It can be used as fertiliser for their plants at the office or at home. Along with food waste, the team also collects coffee grounds that offer a pleasant aroma and can be used as a fertiliser or in ashtrays for extinguishing cigarette butts.

Instead of plastic umbrella jackets distributed on rainy days that are usually tossed after a single use, ICC offers an umbrella dryer that can absorb up to five litres of water. It also makes reusable shopping bags available to tenants and guests to discourage plastic and paper bag usage.

For tenants who drive to work, ICC offers an electric car charging station to encourage tenants to reduce air pollutants by opting for an alternative to gas guzzling vehicles.

These environmental conservation actions have been recognised by the Environmental Campaign Committee and a silver statue was presented to the team at the Hong Kong Awards for Environmental Excellence in 2012.

Universal access is another area where ICC has made great strides to make its facilities available to a wider audience. Disabled lifts are available for wheelchair bound users, while Braille and tactile markings are placed on controls. Dropped kerb crossings are denoted with tactile surfaces at right angles to the street and located opposite each other. Wide turnstiles in lobbies allow wheelchair users to access the lifts just as easily as mobile ones. Assisted listening devices are available to facilitate easier communication with hearing impaired users at concierge desks. Each floor of ICC is equipped with a handicapped washroom, with emergency call bells to summon assistance from outside as well as alerting the control room. In addition, Braille and tactile information on directional arrows are on

handrails on every floor, with hazard warning tiles on every landing. Since ICC has opened for business, it has won a number of building and facilities management awards. These include four Quality Building Awards in 2012, Hong Kong-BEAM Platinum Standard for environmental performance from Hong Kong-BEAM Society, Grand Award (Office Building) at the Hong Kong Institute of Facility Management's Excellence in Facility Management Award in 2012, and Quality Property and Facility Management Awards 2012 presented by the Hong Kong Association of Property Management Company and the Hong Kong Institute of Surveyors. In addition, the Royal Institution of Chartered Surveyors also presented the team with the Property Management Team of the Year Grand Award in 2013.

Opposite page: The gondola cleaning system viewed from the roof of ICC.

Above, top: ICC's double decker lift system is secured with a personal card-based turnstile system to allow restricted access to every level.

Above, bottom: A view down one of ICC's lift shafts.

To the Lighthouse

With Hirohito Totsune, President, Sirius Lighting

Every evening, the façade of ICC is transformed into a tapestry of moving lights that tell a uniquely Hong Kong story. Lighting designer Hirohito Totsune was responsible for the visual feast.

Hong Kong's skyline is one of the most recognisable in the world. The city's identity is intrinsically linked to the stretch of architecture along its waterfront. At dusk, the skyline undergoes a remarkable change as colourful lights transform buildings into a visual smorgasbord. The combination of sky, sea, mountains and high rises never fail to impress even the most jaded of visitors or residents.

Sun Hung Kai Properties believes that ICC's exterior architectural lighting can accomplish much more than merely help identify the building. To that end, the company sought the assistance of Tokyo-based Sirius Lighting Office to design a seasonal programme for an exterior light show. The ICC Light and Music Show has since been acknowledged as the world's largest light and sound show on a single building, awarded with a Guinness World Record certificate in April 2013. "We envision the show as a gift or attraction for locals and visitors," explains Tony Tang. "They can be entertained as they are dining. The show is not just a pattern or brightness on the building; it is a moving story."

The show takes place rain or shine every evening at 7:45 and 9:00 pm. Its duration is four minutes. It is synchronised to accompanying music which is freely accessible via applications downloadable onto iPhones or android devices. At designated Sun Hung Kai Properties shopping malls such as the podium at International Finance Centre, the music is broadcast. "The show changes each season," notes Cris Fung, Sun Hung Kai Properties Real Estate Agency's general manager of retail marketing and customer relations. "It brings a positive message to Hong Kong audiences. Although the weather may prevent the entire building from being visible, the design of each show is for images to begin at the bottom of the building and move around it to the top, helping to showcase its height. It is about much more than architectural lighting."

To achieve its mandate, Sun Hung Kai Properties looked to Hirohito Totsune for a design solution after researching different companies' portfolios for tall building light solutions. "We flew to Tokyo to meet with him," says Tang. "We only knew previously that his company did Tokyo Sky Tree. But that building's light patterns doesn't move. We knew that ICC's architectural lighting offers a great deal of flexibility. He came back to us with a seasonal concept. We then thought that it could be a show, like a film projected onto the building. He said that a show needed music." In the end, the technology already in place through ICC's light programme allowed Sirius Lighting to implement schemes for images to be represented through tonal changes. By restricting the colour to white light, the different grades of light and shade making up moving images show depth and are akin to watercolour paintings. "Aside from our use of LED lamps, the patterns utilise 40 to 50% of each lamp's capacity," says Fung. "We recognize that as a responsible corporate citizen, our show can also be sustainable."

"Lighting is very important to the psychology of a city," says Tang. "No one understands this better than Hirohito. After the tsunami hit Japan in 2011, Japanese people became very sensitive to how electricity was used. But at the same time, a city's energy and optimism is tied into its nightlife."

Totsune originally majored in architecture at The University of Tokyo. He went on to join Lighting Planners Associates, a renowned Japanese architectural lighting company, for eight years before establishing his own company. After collaborating with Hong Kong-based interior design firm AB Concepts on a proposal for a W Hotel in Yokohama, the two firms began working together on a few Hong Kong projects. He set up a Hong Kong office to better service his Chinese clients, though the bulk of his projects remain in Japan.

"Hong Kong's landscape is full of energy," says Totsune. "We wanted to capture that with a light show that involves a lot of movement, like a film. But it also had to have a human aspect to it, for Hong Kong audiences to relate to the images." The designer faced the challenge of working with a thin, tall canvas for his work along with the many diverse weather conditions that may restrict how much of the tower can be seen. "We did a first draft and tested it on the building," recalls Totsune. "The bad weather meant that the top half of the building was hidden behind clouds. We ended up changing the content to accommodate for rainy or cloudy days, so that people can view it nightly regardless of the weather."

"I believe that using just white light is more artistic," Totsune explains. "Viewers become more sensitive to the images themselves. As the images are moving, they contrast against the tenants and users' lights within the building. The images are projected on three facades of the building as the fourth one faces residential towers. We work with the music that Sun Hung Kai Properties provides to create a new show every three months. ICC is a landmark building in Hong Kong and we hope to provide a show that gives Hong Kong people joy."

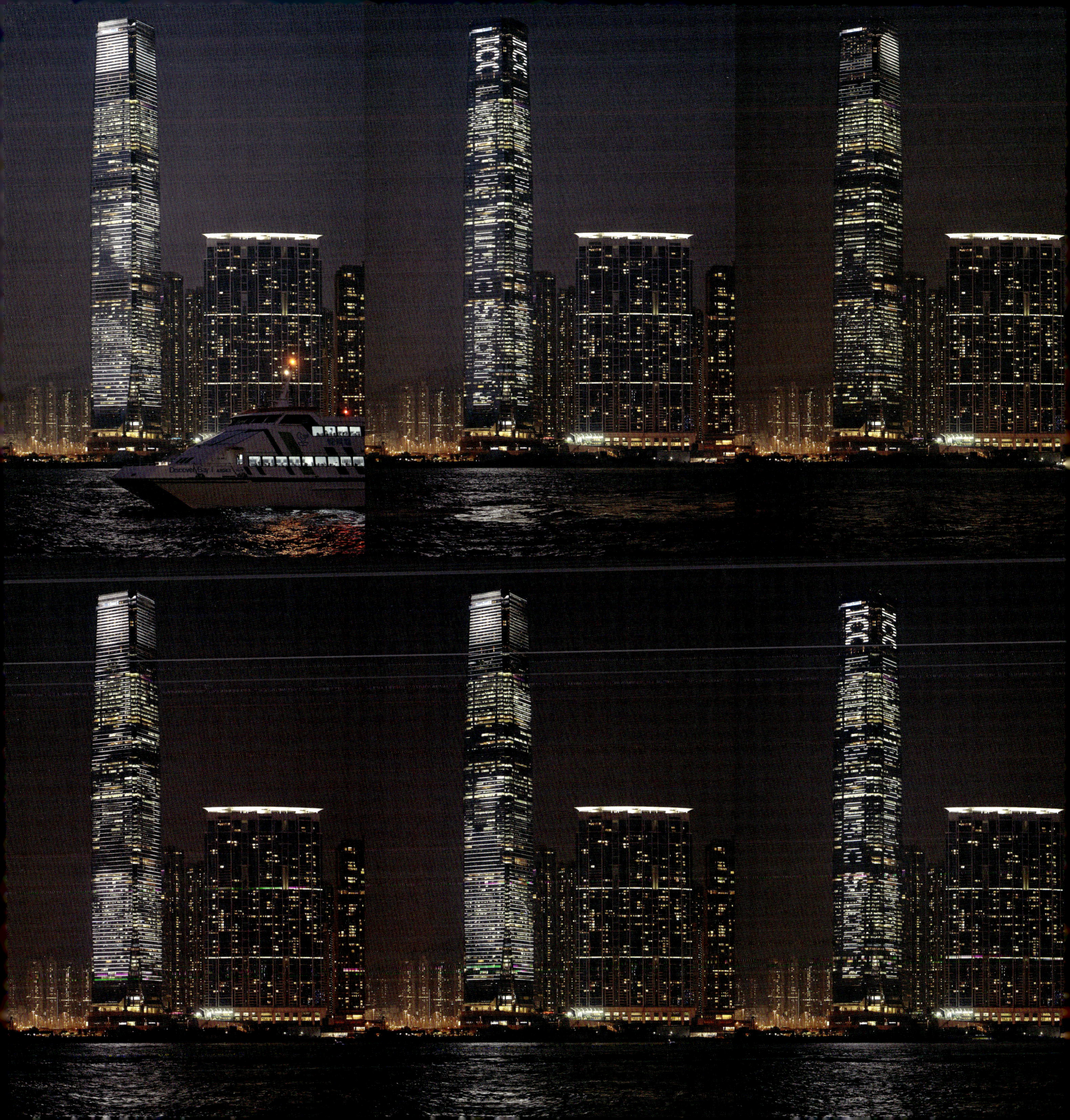

12/

TOUCHING THE SKY

In the few years since ICC has opened, it has already become one of Hong Kong's landmark buildings. Indeed, it is difficult to imagine the skyline without the gently tapering tower at the foot of West Kowloon. Crossing Victoria Harbour on the Star Ferry at night may be one of the best ways to enjoy it, as ICC puts on one of the city's best light shows. Fish swimming upwards morph into Bauhinia flowers blossoming on the three sides of the building, illustrating that it is a blank canvas ready to mirror the city's aspirations.

As West Kowloon evolves, so will ICC. West Kowloon Cultural District will bring yet another audience to the area that will populate it on weekends and weeknights for everything from art exhibitions to international performances. Connectivity will be extended to pedestrian traffic in addition to the vehicular and rail infrastructure already in place. West Kowloon Terminus will usher in a group of savvy travellers to whom time means money. They will look to West Kowloon to fulfill all of their needs within walking distance of the station, and that includes both business and leisure activities. The established neighbourhood of Tai Kok Tsui is slowly transforming to become more eclectic, as some of its walk up tenements are gradually replaced by high rise residences.

Looking into the crystal ball, the future of ICC is fuzzy. The building has adapted to suit its anchor bank tenants, with the ripple effects felt throughout the city as a shift in Central's makeup. Will its evolution be similar to Canary Wharf, La Defense or Pudong? Or will it carve its own path to success? As the structure bends according to the prevailing wind, the vessel that is ICC will be continually replenished with the next wave of financial and economic powerhouses. The elegance of its design beckons intrepid entrepreneurs who believe that ICC and West Kowloon provide a gateway to mainland China. Even years after its opening, its services remain unrivalled in the city and is testament to just how seriously Sun Hung Kai Properties takes its responsibilities as a landlord.

ICC can be viewed as a symbol for the future of Hong Kong. As Kowloon's tenth dragon, it will continue to dominate the skyline for years to come as a gleaming reminder of what is possible.

Preceding pages: During one of Hong Kong's annual festivals, fireworks light up Victoria Harbour and transform the sky into a dazzling theatre of sound and colour.

Opposite page: Like a vessel that takes on its contents' attributes, ICC will continue to evolve as its tenants and the district develops into a true financial neighbourhood.

Right: Under moonlight, ICC resembles a romantic sign post guiding weary travellers into the safety of Victoria Harbour.

Above: The combination of architectural marvels such as ICC against sea, sky and hills make Hong Kong's skyline one of the most iconic in the world.

Opposite page: ICC embraces the challenges that it faces as West Kowloon becomes Hong Kong's gateway.

Following pages: ICC stands tall in the backdrop against the glow of an orange sunset upon Kowloon

SENTINEL OF LIGHT

Joseph Giovannini

In certain lights, at certain times, travellers approaching Hong Kong from the airport glimpse what appears to be a tall wand of light emanating from the tip of Kowloon Peninsula, along Victoria Harbour. By a deliberate act of architectural prestidigitation, the designers of the super tall tower dematerialised the 118-story structure, dissolving its mass, creating spectral façades that seem to live in the sky, reflecting clouds, haze and blue. They designed light.

At a distance, the three-million-square-foot International Commerce Centre reads as a sentinel in the city, soaring above its neighbours. But from other points of view, it couples with Hong Kong's other very tall structure, Two International Finance Centre across the harbour, to form a gateway. In both cases—as sole sentinel and as one leg of a civic gateway—ICC stands out in this city of skyscrapers and high-rises, commanding attention for its scale and attracting attention for its luminous presence. Like ancient Chinese landscape scrolls in which solid mountains dissolve in mists, the tower is almost not there, beguiling for atmospheric reflections of nature's ephemera and for its tendency to disappear into the sky. The building changes before your eyes.

It is sometimes said that super tall towers are more engineered than designed. Perhaps. But in the case of the ICC, engineering and design are interlocked and interdependent, each growing out of the other. In Hong Kong, wind load calculations demanded a stable symmetrical form that would shed vortices and reduce turbulence. For ease of office-floor layout, the developer, Sun Hung Kai Properties, concurred with the engineers, preferring a square-tower format; their commercial requirements agreeing with physics. William Pedersen, lead designer on the project for ICC's design architect Kohn Pedersen Fox, accepted and built on the structural and commercial mandate because he believes: "A building of this type can be perceived as threatening. It's better to err on the side of simplicity and refinement, to dampen the intimidating characteristics of its scale. The very tall building has to be serene, a stabilising rather than agitating force on the skyline." The architecture profession and China have, over the last decade, seen form inflation in highrises. But Pedersen, in Hong Kong as in his super tall predecessor, the World Finance Centre in Shanghai, opted for serenity.

Efficiencies of structure and commerce, then, demanded a square, which the architects would work with to achieve greater efficiency and a strong iconic presence: the tallest building in Hong Kong—one of the tallest in the world—had to live up to its responsibilities as a symbol of one of the world's most dynamic financial centres. Through design, the architects had to refresh and even transcend the typology of a point tower. They had to make convention new.

The first of a few eventful operations that the architects performed on the form of the point tower was to notch its four corners. KPF worked with New York engineers Leslie E. Robertson Associates and Hong Kong based consultants project architect Wong Ouyang and engineer Ove Arup; it found that inverting each corner would confuse and weaken the wind. In Hong Kong typhoons can reach up to 500 km per hour on the top floors—the speed of a plane. The strategy of notching corners also doubled their number, and therefore the commercial potential of the floor plan. The notches themselves transform as they rise, again as a result of wind load considerations. The engineers and architects flared the base out by several degrees and also tapered the top by a degree, where the hotel was to be located. Like a Greek column, the tower acquired a nuanced silhouette: the shaft was not straight but acquired its own subtle version of entasis. The architects and engineers also simplified each floor plate by supporting the perimeter with eight super columns. Between the super columns and service core, the floors are column free.

Besides endowing the simplicity of the 118-story tower with a nuanced shape, the architects pursued elegance as a strategy to mitigate its impact and make the tower into an object the eye wants to see. They rethought the fundamentals of the façade. Because the notched corners broke the volume, and because the super columns were placed inboard from the perimeter, the architects could treat the façade as an independent element sheathing the structure, like the husk of an ear of corn. Divorced from structure, the four façades were even independent of the re-entrant corners, so that each façade could act as a shield independent of the volume itself. The shields were free to slide beyond the volumes to take on roles aside from simple enclosure.

After decades of highrise design, the architects have made a specialty of spatialising façades, of carving surfaces and finding space and the illusion of depth in a matter of inches. The result has been topographic richness, textural weaves of light and shadow playing within rhythmic patterns repeated across the buildings. But in Hong Kong at the ICC, they reinvented even their own specialty by conceiving the glass as more than a plane held flat by the straight mullions of a uniform grid. The panes of glass, designed within a unitised module manufactured off-site, were supported from the back on a steel armature that angled the glass like a shingle, disappearing beneath its surface. What might have been a taut façade instead felt dimensional and open, like gills breathing in the environment. Though notched at the four corners and slightly angled, the form of the tower remained basic, an extrusion from a square plan. But tilting the glass off the vertical like a shingle set the architects off on a chain reaction of design decisions all made to reinforce their intention of making the façade light and airy.

Refinements compounded refinements. The supporting steel armature of each unit was detailed and coloured to disappear into the surrounding reflections: the steel does not invade the shimmer and disturb the reflections. The architects calibrated the degree of reflection to maintain a diaphanous ambiguity between transparency and reflectiveness, one that allowed a clear reading of the forms and shingling without becoming a mirror. The architects chose a low-E glass that reflects out light in the ultraviolet and infrared range but admits light in the visible spectrum, remaining highly transparent from the inside. Wind loads required a thick laminated glass, which added to the reflectivity. The reflectivity was further augmented by the tapering angle of the top third of the tower, programmed for the hotel.

The unitised frame liberated the glass from the mullion system that normally confines glass to a single overall plane. The texture of the shingling allowed the architects to camouflage external louvres necessitated by internalised mechanical floors. The architects boldly striate horizontal bars at two heights on the façade, making graphic the open-air refuge floors required by law: the windowless openings read like minimalist abstractions.

Normally, a detail remains small in scale without impact overall, simply a matter of the way a beam meets a column, or a building turns a corner. The device of angled sheets of glass applied over 118 stories became environmental. A very simple design move to mitigate the basic mass of the building created another reality, fundamentally altering through its cumulative impact the appearance of the entire building. Rather than being an imposing, unchangeable building fixed in its monumentality, the tower became temporal, the atmospheric effects imparting an element of time, change and immateriality to its image. The design eschewed the static for the momentary. In an architectural era characterised by heroic formal gestures, the architects capitalised instead on subtlety, building their design on the cumulative impact of nuance. Successive refinement gave a certain delicacy to a mass that might otherwise have been brutal.

Many super tall buildings, successful in the skyline, have trouble meeting the ground and making the transition from their monumental scale to the pedestrian and vehicular needs of the immediate urban environment. For the architects, one answer to the question of how to negotiate between the vertical and the horizontal lay in their invention of their shingled façades: having broken the prismatic volume at the corners into four separate surfaces, like shields, the architects were able to extend the shields at the tower's base and bend them to cover the surrounding spaces like canopies. They simply peeled the surfaces off from the volume. At the base of the tower the architects extended each façade, flaring each to create micro-environments around the entries that serve as transitional spaces for the surrounding roads. On the east, west and south façades, the façades escape the volume in a graceful flow of glass that hovers over arriving cars. Without being literal or culturally sentimental, the architects designed the cantilevered steel frames holding the glass shingles to suggest entrance gates to traditional Chinese palaces and temples. Like porches, they frame views out to Victoria Harbour and Hong Kong's mountainous landscape.

Given the independence of each façade from the other, the architects do not have to treat each the same way. On the north façade, the architects break the symmetry and extend the façade dramatically into what they call "the dragon's tail," a long extrusion of steel and glass that thrusts toward a public plaza ringed by restaurants serving the ICC and surrounding buildings. Reinforcing the metaphor of the dragon's tail is the shingles' resemblance to the scales of a dragon's skin.

Between the dragon tail and traditional gates, the visual references to Chinese lore and culture bridge Hong Kong's contemporary and traditional worlds, ingratiating the building to the collective cultural awareness of residents: the references make the building more familiar and comfortable. The international building is, in a subliminal way, local.

While the tower succeeds as an understated icon in the skyline, it rests on a podium and can also be understood as an outgrowth of Kowloon's newly upgraded subterranean infrastructure. Beneath the glazed dragon's tale, banks of escalators lead down to a large shopping mall, Elements, and on to Hong Kong's infrastructure of transport— the metro system, the airport train, and the rail network connecting Hong Kong to mainland China.

Again the architectural typology, a podium supporting a tower, is a familiar one, but the podium here is especially complex and layered, on many floors. The base has to accommodate roadways, parking, bus transport, shopping, and tour groups, not to mention some 25,000 people who enter and exit the building daily. The podium translates horizontal circulation to vertical by separating arrivals and departures on several floors, where double deck elevators with destination control whisk people to designated floors. The unseen anatomy of the building is especially complex at the intersections of the horizontal and vertical transportation systems.

An event on the skyline, the tower has the mass of an iceberg below grade, where it ties in efficiently and directly to the public transportation that is diversifying Hong Kong's traditional orientation beyond Central. Invigorated by the new airport rail line and the future bullet train from Beijing, Shanghai and Guangzhou, plus new building heights permitted by decommissioning the old Kowloon airport, Kowloon is becoming a second CBD for Hong Kong, with ICC as its hub. The tower is not only a destination site and symbol of the city, but the summary building in Hong Kong's expanding and shifting new urban plan. The success of the tower and the CBD depends on the permeability of the membrane between the tower and the supporting infrastructure. The tower is designed to root deeply into the city's new urbanism, drawing on the local, regional and national energies that course through its systems, establishing a model of sustainability as a highrise integrated into its urban environment. The ICC also pivots Kowloon toward the future West Kowloon Cultural District, masterplanned by Foster + Partners, on reclaimed land adjacent to the complex. ICC is not an isolated monument, but is rooted in the forces of Hong Kong's future. The developer and team responded as carefully to the urban links below grade as they did to the structural engineering in the visible portions of the tower. The tower is embedded as a vital component in an emerging ecosystem.

ICC is one of an emerging class of super tall towers now marking, or rising in, many Asian cities. But height alone in this competitive arena no longer automatically singles out a building and city, commanding respect and awe. Engineering and impressive statistics do not necessarily make one super tall building better than another. China, in its quest for status as a first-world country, and Hong Kong, in its civic competition with other financial hubs like Singapore and Shanghai, are putting an increasing emphasis on both the quality of construction and the elegance of concept. What earns the ICC its place in this arena of competing financial city states is its close symbiotic relationship between structure and design: the elegant engineering solution was absorbed in an architectural concept that contextualised the engineering in an unusual vision that was skillfully realised. Engineering and architecture, insofar as they can be dissociated from one another in the reflexive process of the building's creation, are mutually supportive and integrated, like the design of a high performance plane or car.

The power of the building, then, resides in the design's inseparable relationship between engineering and architecture. The engineering was determinant, but the design, transformative. Each grew from the other in this 118-story intersection of art and technology. Each gave the other value.

Joseph Giovannini Trained at Harvard as an architect, Joseph Giovannini has written as a critic and author on architecture since the early 1980s, covering architecture and design for The Los Angeles Herald Examiner, The New York Times, and New York Magazine. He has also written for many professional journals, including Architect Magazine, Architectural Record and Progressive Architecture, and frequently contributes essays for museum catalogues and architectural monographs. He practices architecture in New York and Los Angeles, and specializes in converting industrial structures into residential lofts. He is currently finishing a book on the history of Deconstructivism, to be published by Rizzoli in 2015.

THE LITTLE ISLAND THAT COULD

Edwin Heathcote

If a city's skyline is the measure of its energy, like an electrocardiograph of its economic and cultural pulse, then Hong Kong is bursting with life. Its skyline is hypertrophied, a graphic of ambition, success and an extraordinary ability to adapt, absorb and change. No other city can match it. New York, the city most associated with the skyscraper, has less than half as many tall buildings as Hong Kong, Tokyo a little more than a quarter. The little island on the southern edge of China has made the porcupine skyline its own and its architecture, en masse, has become its spectacle.

In which other city do crowds gather in the evening to admire architecture and urbanism, as they do at the Star Ferry Terminal to watch the kitschy, twinkling illuminations of the skyscrapers on the other side? Tall towers in Hong Kong have become a modernist vernacular, an expression of density and the huge land values created by the constrictive natural boundary of the sea.

The irony, of course, is that those crowds flock to the other side of the harbour, to Kowloon, from where the spectacle of the sparkling towers can best be seen. The spectacle can always be best observed at a slight remove, across the water where the towers and their illuminations are reflected and refracted in the waters. The southern tip of the mainland part of Hong Kong, Tsim Sha Tsui, has increasingly itself become a destination, a super-dense district, a symptom of the skyscraper and shopping effect radiating across from the island. But Kowloon has its own unique history of density and an architecture as distinctive as that over the water. Its walled city, the last dark alleys of which disappeared than two decades ago, was an almost unimaginably dense and intense fragment of urbanity and the teeming markets of Mong Kok still reveal a bustling indigenous trade culture in which architecture is packed so tight it becomes almost impossible to see except in its details.

Hong Kong's colonial history has cast a long shadow over its present - and its future, but that shadow has been part cool shade and part darkness. Its real estate was, and still is, locked into a colonial demarcation which defines Central as its business district and the Peak as its cool suburban retreat. Everything else has been treated as somehow inferior and even decades of redevelopment around its seemingly endless docks hasn't quite dented the primacy of that colonial real estate legacy.

But now, perhaps, things are finally changing and it is characteristic of Hong Kong that it should be a skyscraper that marks the moment. The completion of Hong Kong's tallest tower, the ICC, in 2012 is a manifestation of the shift, a graphic representation of a real estate upheaval which had been happening for many years but which was only crystallised in the consciousness of the city by the appearance of this sleek, 118 storey tower.

The end of the era which occurred at the handover in 1994 saw the shift in power and influence from faraway Britain and the island's history, to the neighbouring emerging industrial and economic superpower China - and Hong Kong's future.

That shift has already been amplified by the construction of the MTR High Speed Airport Express which whisks visitors into Kowloon Station in twenty minutes in one of the easiest and most seamless transitions form international terminal to city anywhere in the world. And that train takes passengers right into the bowels of the complex that is crowned by the tower. Visitors emerge from Sir Terry Farrell's impressively engineered subterranean megastructure in the elegant Elements mall, a swirling interior landscape of light stone floors and global brands displayed in shiny shopfronts.

But even this most dramatic of arrivals marks only the beginning. Just behind the site, West Kowloon is, at the time of writing, being churned up as a massive new station is being carved out to link Hong Kong with the big, booming industrial cities of mainland China. Above it is fast emerging the West Kowloon Cultural Centre, an ambitious arts behemoth for a city in which culture had traditionally been left behind in the wake of commerce. The arts centre, masterplanned by Foster & Partners, promises another radical and very visible shift from the island to Kowloon. With buildings attempting to embrace all art forms from traditional Chinese and western opera through fine art and design, it is intended to finally establish Hong Kong as the cultural capital it has never been.

The new station meanwhile will fundamentally alter the dynamic of the city, creating an umbilical link to the industrial and financial centres of the booming mainland. The big manufacturing cities of Shenzhen, Guangzhou and the Pearl River Delta began taking over from Hong Kong as China's industrial base in the 1970s and have since developed into the world's production hub. The high speed rail link currently under construction will effectively create a single, huge networked city, of which Hong Kong will be the trading, commercial and international heart in a way that mainland China cannot yet quite be. Beyond that it will make Beijing accessible in a manner that the current air links do not quite achieve, it will achieve a synthesis of Hong Kong and China in a manner that has never quite occurred since the handover. Kowloon, always the bridge between the mainland and the island will become even more of a fulcrum.

The ICC building, soaring over the hub of the unfolding viscera of the rapidly expanding rail network, has already become a symbol of that emergence. Only a few years ago it would have been unthinkable for major banks to relocate from Central to Kowloon. The nickname 'The Dark Side' was a veiled joke concealing a truth, within it lay a sharp rebuke to Kowloon's ambitions. Yet here is a building clad entirely in high-tech shimmering glass, rising to 484m, a symmetrical riposte to its aesthetic twin, the 420m IFC Building on the other side of Victoria Harbour. It is a building intended at least in part, to dispel any notions of darkness. Every aspect of the tower seems to reinforce its image as a beacon for a new quarter. Its glazed façade sweeps down to meet the ground in a curving canopy which embraces the ground beneath it as well as the subterranean realms yet further below. In bringing the intermediate lobby, transport interchange and shopping realms together in a generous public space at its base it also does something which few Hong Kong buildings are able – it brings in light from above through the lofty glass roof formed by the curve of the façade.

The confluence of functions at the base of the building creates and nurtures an urbanity based on a mix of uses which keeps the space busy through all times of the day, a series of parallel city cycles which animate the architecture through daylight and night-time. The emulation of a dragon's scales in the way the façade peels off the tower to become a canopy to the public space is also a kind of architecture parlante. The canted struts supporting it reinforce the directionality of the space and impart a dynamism as does the sweep of the roof which echoes the movement of the escalators which create the critical link between the horizontal strata of the centre, the transport, retail, urban and commercial. That sweeping canopy gushes out from the vertical surface of the tower toward the water as it appears to reconcile the tower and the plane of the sea.

The space below becomes a mini metropolis, a place in which the height of the tower illustrates an intensification of an emerging contemporary urbanity on the Kowloon side. It is that urbanity and intensity which has lured the big banks to establish their HQs here in a move that would have been unthinkable before the tower was conceived. To have attracted Morgan Stanley, Deutsche Bank and Credit Suisse over the water is an extraordinary coup and a testament to the power of architecture to create a place. When HSBC commissioned Foster and Partners to design their HQ in 1978, it represented a moment in which Hong Kong recognised the potential of a building to encapsulate the image of an institution and a place within the crowded skyline and the busy streets. It was the most expensive building in the world when it was completed yet Foster carved space out underneath the building to create a public plaza and a dramatic urban moment at street level as well as at the level of the city panorama. I.M. Pei was more traditional in his bank of China building which is elegant and extremely tall (and with a consequent distinctive structural character on the skyline) but is less generous at ground level. Its moment is at high level.

Kohn Pedersen Fox's ICC Tower appears to amalgamate both approaches. Its profile is distinctive – if not expressionistically so and the architectural language in which it is expressed is spare but sophisticated, part of a very different world to that of the more self-consciously expressive towers on the island side which collectively compose the night-time skyline illuminations. Dennis Lau and Ng Chun Man's towers, Central Plaza and The Center, both refer to a US tradition of the extended shaft and the feature crown, with its distinctive set-backs and pyramidal forms commisioned by Sun Hung Kay Properties. Kohn Pedersen Fox, despite being based in New York, have been careful to avoid that kind of historicising reference, instead turning to a pared-back language in which the building is defined by the subtle profile and its thoughtful details; the way the façade peels away at the edges at the top and bottom, the way the canopy sweeps down towards the sea, the way in which the tower appears to taper top and bottom.

The ICC has been conceived very deliberately as a twin to the IFC Tower, also developed by Sun Hung Kai Properties. The two towers on opposite sides of the harbour are intended to create the effect of a gateway, the twin posts of a grand waterborne entrance to the Fragrant Harbour. Their forms echo each other closely, both subtly tapering towards the sky and both implying, rather than explicitly expressing the classic skyscraper form of base, shaft and crown. But the subtle variations between them also reveal something about the two sites.

The IFC Tower, designed by Cesar Pelli, tapers through a series of diminishing setbacks. The effect is reminiscent of Pelli's best Art Deco and Post Modern-inflected buildings which imparts it a slightly North American air. It has a hint of Chicago or New York about it, the stepped language of the inter-war classic skyscraper and, like those buildings, it terminates in an openwork crown, a kind of comb. The ICC Tower meanwhile is smoother, more seamless and its skin seems more applied. The elevations appear as membranes applied to the tower's four facades yet the corners remain visible behind them. The effect is to reduce the mass and the bulk of the building, to dematerialise its edges. The same technique is used at the top of the building so that by gradually reducing the width of the glass curtain wall the top seems to disappear into the sky as it the tower gently tapers. The effect is felt most clearly at night when the illuminated corners of the tower illustrate the membrane-like nature of the cladding to the four faces and the tower glows in fine lines as it rises.

The location of the Ritz Carlton Hotel on the top floors of the tower – making this the tallest hotel in the world – adds another level of intensification to the building. Already animated by the public space of the Sky 100 observation lobby on the 100th floor, a viewing gallery and tourist attraction which offers panoramic views of the harbour – the hotel creates a series of restaurants and public and semi-public spaces at the top of the building which draws urban life up right through its entire height. The height of the tower functions like a pin in a map, focussing attention on a spot, drawing the eye to the shifting centre of gravity of Hong Kong. But its aesthetic partnering with the ICC Tower across the water allows the building to becomes something more than a single marker. The twinning of the towers creates an equivalence and a dialogue across the harbour, a parity between the Island and Kowloon which acts as an architectural and urban device to tie the two together whilst also marking them individually. A tower on its own can become a self-conscious icon, a gesture of self-importance, but in this way, as part of a pair it becomes much more of an urban gesture, something relating to the changing nature of the city, the shifting emphasis of place and trade, of value and connections. The ICC Tower acts to express the emergence of a new hub, a place which bonds Hong Kong more tightly to the mainland both physically and metaphorically whilst simultaneously expressing through its architectural quality and its sleek elegance the difference in sophistication and thoughtful design between the Hong Kong skyline and the brasher, quicker, less considered skylines of the booming nearby Pearl River Delta.

The twin towers on either side of the harbour represent the apex of developer SKHP's long history of building Hong Kong's most notable high rises. For the last four decades their towers have punctured the island's spiky skyline, with a series of towers which have been amongst the tallest of their time. The sleek, black tower of the Sun Hung Kai Properties Centre in Wan Chai set the scene for the 1980s. Central Plaza (also in Wan Chai), with its New York style crown took over from I.M. Pei's bank of China Tower as the island's tallest building in the 1990s and in the 2000s KPF's IFC tower became the island's tallest (and the world's fourth tallest) skyscraper. Through each of these towers the articulation has become more important and more sophisticated so that each era has its symbol and the skyline becomes finer and more complex, rather than just a jostling crowd of extruded blocks. SKHP's approach has been increasingly to use architecture both as landmark and hook to draw tenants in and retain them. There is a dedication to both skyline and street and an acknowledgment of the particular blend of features which make a building desirable to the major financial companies who form the backbone of their business. That mix includes a landmark tower with a presence on the skyline, a place to act as symbol and sign; views to take advantage of the island's spectacular setting and skyline; good transport links and a central location; a lively, generous lobby; high quality office space and, finally, an integration into the buzzing streets below.

At the time of writing, the ICC and its surroundings are not quite that finished piece of urbanity. Rather it is an elegant tower pitched into a still unresolved landscape. It is true that the view from the plaza in front of the Ritz Carlton's reception offers perhaps the most breathtaking and complete panorama of Hong Kong that can be had from sea level. And it is the case that arrival into the subterranean Kowloon Station and the emergence into the sleek space of the Elements mall is a seamless experience. But it is also worth pointing out that the area behind the development is in a state of churn. The whole ensemble will only be ready to be judged when the new station and the West Kowloon Arts Centre are fully developed and functioning, a moment which is likely to truly transform the physical and psychological topography of Hong Kong. Until then however, the attenuated form of the ICC Tower marks this out as the place to watch. Hong Kong is changing and the most eloquent and elegant expression of that change is the city tallest building.

Edwin Heathcote is an architect, designer and writer living and working in London. He is the architecture critic of The Financial Times and the author of around a dozen books including 'The Meaning of Home' and 'The Architecture of Hope'. He writes a monthly column for GQ Magazine and is a regular contributor to a number of architecture and design journals. He is a contributing editor for ICON Magazine and on the editorial board of Architectural Design. Heathcote is currently establishing an online archive of critical writing on design.

CONTRIBUTORS

KEVIN CHAN
Originally from Hong Kong and a long time resident of Canada, Kevin is a private investment banker and resident at Sorrento at West Kowloon, where he lives with his family.

JOSEPH GIOVANNINI
Trained at Harvard as an architect, Joseph has written as a critic and author on architecture since the early 1980s, covering architecture and design for The Los Angeles Herald Examiner, The New York Times, and New York Magazine. He has also written for many professional journals, including Architect Magazine, Architectural Record and Progressive Architecture, and frequently contributes essays for museum catalogues and architectural monographs. He practises architecture in New York and Los Angeles and specialises in converting industrial structures into residential lofts. He is currently finishing a book on the history of Deconstructivism, to be published by Rizzoli in 2015.

EDWIN HEATHCOTE
Edwin is an architect, designer and writer living and working in London. He is the architecture critic of The Financial Times and the author of around a dozen books including The Meaning of Home and The Architecture of Hope. He writes a monthly column for GQ Magazine and is a regular contributor to a number of architecture and design journals. He is a contributing editor for ICON Magazine and on the editorial board of Architectural Design. He is currently establishing an online archive of critical writing on design.

PAUL LAU
Michelin-starred Chef Paul Lau Ping Lui is regarded as one of the top Cantonese chefs in Hong Kong. He has over 34 years of experience in Chinese culinary arts, which he honed from working in far-flung Johannesburg and Dubai, along with some of mainland China's best hotels. He has been Chef de Cuisine at The Ritz-Carlton, Hong Kong's Tin Lung Heen since the restaurant first opened in 2011, winning the restaurant one Michelin star in 2012 and two Michelin stars in 2013, 2014 and 2015.

DAVID LUNG
Lady Edith Kotewall Professor in the Built Environment and Dean of Architecture at The University of Hong Kong, David is internationally recognised for his work in heritage conservation and World Heritage properties. He was instrumental in bringing to fruition three World Heritage Inscriptions: Historic City of Macao, Kaiping Diaolou and Villages, and the Historic Cities in the Straits of Malacca. He started HKU's Architectural Conservation Programme in 2000 and set up an architectural conservation laboratory in teaching and researching on historic building materials in 2012, enabling collaborative research and bringing together a multi-disciplinary research team in providing expert knowledge and service for conservation projects in Hong Kong. He has served in the public built environment sector, holding key positions including chairman of the Antiquities Advisory Board and non-executive Director of the Urban Renewal Authority.

VALERIE PORTEFAIX
Originally from France and trained as an architect, Valerie Portefaix and her husband and business partner Laurent Gutierrez have been based in Hong Kong since 1996, where they founded MAP Office, a multidisciplinary platform using varied means of expression including drawing, photography, video, installations, performance, and literary and theoretical texts. MAP's projects form a critique of spatial-temporal anomalies and documents how human beings subvert and appropriate space. MAP's exhibition Hong Kong is Land was exhibited at MoMA in 2014-15 as part of Uneven Growth: Tactical Urbanisms for Expanding Megacities. Valerie is a lecturer at Hong Kong Polytechnic University's School of Design, Master of Design programme.

KEN SHUTTLEWORTH
Ken is an English architect who worked on Hong Kong's HSBC Headquarters and Hong Kong International Airport while he was a partner with Foster and Partners. He founded Make Architects in 2004 and the firm currently has studios in London, Beijing and Hong Kong. Make, a 100% employee owned organisation with a flat corporate structure, works on

a broad selection of projects worldwide, ranging from large-scale urban masterplans to luxury private houses. Make's projects include The Copper Box, built for London's 2012 Olympics for handball competition, The Temple House for Swire Hotels in Chengdu and HSBC Quai des Bergues in Geneva.

ARTUR C.K. AU-YEUNG is Director with Wong & Ouyang

MARGARET P.L. CHAN is Senior Development Manager – Planning, Project Planning & Development Department with Sun Hung Kai Properties

CRIS Y.L. FUNG is General Manager, Retail Marketing and Customer Relations, Leasing Department with Sun Hung Kai Properties Real Estate Agency

PHILIP LAI is Director with Arup

AUGUSTINE T.S. LEE is an architect and Project Director with Sun Hung Kai Properties

K.W. LO is General Manager – Leasing, Office Leasing Department with Sun Hung Kai Properties Real Estate Agency

TIM M.T. MAK is an Authorised Person, Registered Architect and Assistant Project Director, Special Projects Department with Sun Hung Kai Properties

DAVID MALOTT is Principal with KPF

KENNETH K.F. MO is an Authorised Person, Registered Structural Engineer and General Manager with Sanfield (Management)

TONY W.M. TANG is Deputy Project Director with Harbour Vantage Management

HIROHITO TOTSUNE is President with Sirius Lighting

IRENE WAI is General Manager with International Commerce Centre

H.K. YUNG Is Director with J. Roger Preston

ACKNOWLEDGEMENTS

AECOM Asia Co Ltd

Aedas Ltd

ALT Cladding & Design Philippines Inc

Andrew Lau & Associates (China) Ltd

Architectural Lighting (HK) Limited

Arnhold & Company Limited

ARUP Fire

Asia Sign Engineering Co., Ltd.

ASSA ABLOY Hospitality Limited

ATAL Engineering Ltd.

B.S.C. Interior Contract and Engineering Company Limited

B.S.C. Sanitarywares Supply Limited

Belt Collins Hong Kong Ltd

C&A Design Limited

Campbell Shillinglaw Lau Ltd

Chan & Wong Architects and Engineers Ltd

Chevalier (Aluminium Engineering) Hong Kong Ltd.

China Construction Third Engineering Bureau-Hip Hing Joint Venture

China-Tech Engineering Company Limited

Clover Architectural Design Ltd

CPP Wind Engineering Consultants

Creative Kitchen Planners Inter. Sdn Bhd

Dandy Interior Products Ltd.

Davis Langdon & Seah HK Ltd

Decca (HK) Limited

Design Link Company Limited

Draughtzman

E.W. Cox Hong Kong Limited

ESPA

Everfield Engineering Co. Ltd.

Frost Design Pty Ltd

Fuji (China) Decoration & Engineering Company Limited

Great Treasure International Limited

Gresh Productions sarl

Helicon Ma Surveying Ltd

Hirsch Bedner And Associates Limited

HKU of Science & Technology

Hong Chui Landscape Co Ltd

Hong Kong Telecommunications (HKT) Limited

In Yam Development Ltd

Interior Contract International Limited

J. Roger Preston Ltd

James Law Cybertecture Int Holding Ltd

Johnson Controls Hong Kong Limited

Junefair Engineering Co. Ltd.

Kaba Limited

Kohn Pedersen Fox Associates PC

Kwong Kam Tim Marble Company Limited

Laservision Limited

LERA

LG Electronics HK Limited

Liesse Production Limited

Lim Teo + Wilkes Design Works Ptd Ltd

LPA Lighting Planners Associates Inc

Markasia (Hong Kong) Limited

Maunsell Consultants Asia Ltd

Mechtler (Far East) Limited

MVA Hong Kong Ltd

New Waly Interior Products (HK) Limited

Nixon Technology Co. Ltd.

Ove Arup & Partners HK Ltd

Permasteelisa Hong Kong Limited

Plan In Interior & Contracting Co. Ltd.

PolyU Technology & Consultancy Co Ltd

Poolmate Engineering Co., Ltd.

Pro-United Technology & Engineering Ltd

Radnor Limited

Ricardo Lighting Company Limited

Ridgid Plumbing Ltd.

Rowan Williams Davies & Irwin Inc

Sabrina Fung Fine Arts Ltd

Schindler Lift (HK) Ltd.

Sealy Asia (Hong Kong) Ltd

Shen Milsom Wilke

Shinryo Corporation

SPIN

Sun Hung Kai Architects And Engineers Ltd

SUNeVision Super e-Technology Services Limited

Superview & Co

Takasago Thermal Engineering (HK) Co., Ltd.

The Hong Kong and China Gas Co. Ltd.

The Jardine Engineering Corporation, Limited

Tino Kwan Lighting Consultants Ltd

TMA Transport Planning

United Reliance Corporation Ltd.

Urbis Limited

VSC Building Products Company Limited

Walsh Greene Art Consultancy

Wing Shing Engineering International Co., Ltd.

Wong & Ouyang (HK) Ltd

WSP Hong Kong Ltd

WT Partnership (HK) Ltd

Yue Po Engineering Company Limited